Managing Change

ESSENTIALS OF NURSING MANAGEMENT

Annabel Broome: Managing Change, 2nd edition
Principles of complex change
Leadership and creating change from within
Imposed change
The nurse as a change agent
Identifying training and development needs
Appendices

June Girvin: Leadership and Nursing
The development of theories of leadership
Interpretations of leadership
Interpersonal skills and leadership
Leadership and nursing
The story so far...
Traditional attitudes and socialisation
Motivation
Leadership today
Vision - foresight, insight and dreams

Diana Sale: Quality Assurance, 2nd edition
An introduction to quality assurance
Total Quality Management
Standards of care
Clinical audit
Clinical protocols
Monitoring of providers by purchasers

Verena Tschudin *with* **Jane Schober: Managing Yourself, 2nd edition**
'Know thyself'
Valuing yourself
Motivating yourself
Asserting yourself
Stressing yourself
Supporting yourself
Celebrating yourself
Developing yourself and your career

Geoffrey Woodhall and Alan Stuttard: Financial Management
An introduction to finance in the health service
The planning and control of capital expenditure
Methods of capital appraisal
Sources of capital finance
The planning and control of revenue expenditure
Setting a budget for the first time
Monitoring of budget performance
Putting it all together
Glossary
Appendices

ESSENTIALS OF NURSING MANAGEMENT

Managing Change

2nd Edition

Annabel Broome

First edition 1990
Reprinted five times
Second edition 1998

Published by
PALGRAVE MACMILLAN
Houndmills, Basingstoke, Hampshire RG21 6XS and
175 Fifth Avenue, New York, N. Y. 10010
Companies and representatives throughout the world

PALGRAVE MACMILLAN is the global academic imprint of the Palgrave Macmillan division of St. Martin's Press, LLC and of Palgrave Macmillan Ltd. Macmillan® is a registered trademark in the United States, United Kingdom and other countries. Palgrave is a registered trademark in the European Union and other countries.

ISBN 0–333–67736–6

This book is printed on paper suitable for recycling and made from fully managed and sustained forest sources.

A catalogue record for this book is available from the British Library.

10   9   8   7   6   5
07   06   05   04   03   02

Printed and bound in Great Britain by
Antony Rowe Ltd, Chippenham and Eastbourne

Contents

Acknowledgements

Every effort has been made to trace all the copyright-holders of material used in this book, but if any have been inadvertently overlooked the publishers will be pleased to make the necessary arrangement at the first opportunity.

Introduction

In today's increasingly uncertain and turbulent times, organizations must depend on the people in their systems to develop a culture of innovation and change. It is people who will push for change – not systems or technology. Such hallowed institutions as the NHS cannot remain untouched by the turbulence of the world in general, rapid changes in information technology and changing work patterns.

These factors cause opportunities and tensions for any organization. But for The NHS, which is a deeply traditional and professionally divided institution, there are particular difficulties in responding to these changes. For instance, public demands for health care are changing, and are putting different demands on the style and type of health services. These new demands and new techniques are forcing health services to come to terms with change. Broome[1] outlines some of the influences that are prompting such changes, which include the public's increasing concern with self-care, their demands for more information about treatment options and outcomes, and the Patient's Charter.[2] It is such influences that have an effect on health care and the role of managers who work in them and try to change them.

The new NHS, in creating a market place, is separating the purchasing of services from its delivery, so the contracting and monitoring of services is another pressure for change.

This book is concerned with methods of change, helping the reader to take advantage of these new pressures and new demands, and turning what might be seen as a threat, into an opportunity – because one thing is certain, change is here to stay!

This book has been published in this context of much imposed change. Things have changed somewhat since the first edition: the pressures have increased, the accountabilities have increased and cost consciousness has increased, as well as many changes which simply continue. The book aims to help you to capitalize on this changing climate, taking advantage of the energy this generates, not all of it positive. It will also help the reader to take a step-by-step approach to designing and managing particular changes.

The Current Climate in the NHS

For this second edition, there is a much stronger focus on the recent NHS changes or 'reforms', which have made all professionals aware of the division into purchasers and providers, and have necessitated different structural approaches to deliver to tighter contracts.

This book describes change methodology, and uses examples from the author's current practice and experience. It attempts to bring the theory to life and to make the methods relevant to the NHS and to nurse managers in particular. Towards this end there are brief exercises, to test the usefulness of techniques which should help in the diagnosis of current problems and issues, and demonstrate possible steps in interventions. For the learners or aspiring managers reading the book, it should give a flavour of the issues in the service currently, and the methods they may find others around them using. At the very least, it should leave all readers with a clearer understanding of the broader context of their work and some ways of leading and contributing to the changes.

What is a Healthy Organization?

Knowing what a healthy organization is gives us something to measure ourselves against, as well as something to strive for. At its worst, such an insight may demonstrate that we belong to a sickly system and that the changes needed are so radical that we may consider the struggle too costly to bother with.

So what do we know about healthy systems? We know that some organizations are fitter at sustaining the dynamic environment, an empowered culture, one that can adapt and change to new demands. Individual readers are bound to come from a wide variety of environments: some will be lucky enough to belong to highly adaptive, renewing organizations, though others will be in organizations that struggle to remain untouched and resist each change imposed upon them.

Pedlar's[3] *The Learning Company* has developed the notion of a learning organization, one which constantly adapts, monitors and uses feedback data, and learns from experience.

Rosabeth Kanter's[4] *The Change Masters* describes a handful of important US companies which she rates on the 'innovation index'. She finds that, in the lower-rated group, organizations still demonstrate some innovation, but they tended to have the 'sinking ship' flavour. In the NHS, we can recognize these. They take negative solutions rather than developing a renewing system or learning community. Kanter lists features of less innovative organizations as:

● having strong vertical relationships.
● a lack of resources, to handle both change and routine tasks.

1. Having strong vertical relationships

In the NHS, we see strong hierarchical structures, and the nursing profession is one example, with communication often being highly formalized. This can lead to a lack of co-operation and communication across professions, and prolonged decision-making – passing decisions upwards, across, then down for implementation.

How often do we see ideas being exchanged between people who are from different professions and different hierarchies? People will have difficulty fertilizing new ideas if these hierarchies are too tight. They will have difficulty networking or joining in flexible projects if the hierarchy is tightly and formally controlled. This factor will encourage territorial behaviour and guarding of information. These behaviours can be readily

3

recognized as 'tribalism' and ritualized conflict over territories. Readers may have heard of locality teams endlessly discussing who is the right professional to be key worker to a mentally ill person in the community: is it the community psychiatric nurse, the social worker, the psychologist or the psychiatrist? Such a discussion usually focuses less on identifying the person with the skill or relationship than on the professional territory or role that person occupies. The formal structures that have been adopted recently can either increase this competitiveness and guarding of information, or provide the opportunity to break down territorial or professional boundaries, by setting up cross-agency community teams, for instance.

Efforts at skill mixing are now blurring these boundaries somewhat, and the notion of the generic community nurse appeals particularly to GPs, who see it offering flexibility, closer teamworking and greater accountability to themselves.

The new cost consciousness has also led to a more flexible focus on costings and the identification of competencies, from whichever profession. This has meant, at times, a more competitive price for services, and a more flexible attitude to traditional professional territories. An example of this would be the merging of nursing roles in primary care, often the District nurse and Practice nurse and Health Visitor exchanging roles and duties.

As an example of these issues, I witnessed a discussion between an acute Trust manager and senior professionals, who were discussing how to increase day case surgery, which would increase efficiency and decrease costs per operation and therefore put them in a better position competitively to gain contracts. However, it would also increase demand for out-of-hours home visiting by community nurses. This latter point was not considered as relevant in the contracting because the bill would be picked up by the community Trust, and not by the acute Trust.

Another example, in Obstetrics and Gynaecology, might be useful. In one acute Trust strong competition had been encouraged between two teams which were staffed and managed separately. The team allegiance to each was so strong that scarce items of equipment, which were meant to be shared, were hidden, to make the other team look less efficient in their activity returns. This was putting overall efficiency, and even lives, at risk by structuring the two teams to be so competitive. This example highlights the dangerous aspects of encouraging territorial and exclusive behaviour and the problems of separate contracting for care that should be seamless from a patient's point of view.

Such isolation of professions or cliques, or indeed of Trust Boards, can lose the impetus of full multidisciplinary discussion; and the opportunity both to review current performance in relation to the end customer, the patient, and to develop problem-finding behaviour across the whole episode of care. All these factors are more evident in renewing organizations, which take time and energy to review and adapt appropriately.

2. Increased resources are needed to handle both change and routine tasks

Beckhard[5] has always promoted the idea that the change state is a different state and needs more resources. However some might argue with this, and also about the extent of resource that is needed. I have no doubt additional resources are needed to provide the considerable time and skill for making particular changes. Later in the book the detailed reasons why we need these resources to manage change will become clearer, but in summary, we need additional resources to manage the present at the same time as leading the process of transition: it is necessary to 'mind the shop', while servicing the change.

There are many examples of change projects that simply have not been given the additional resources to manage the change effort. Indeed, one of the commonest resource problems in the NHS is the lack of expertise and numbers in middle management.

Healthy Organizations

Healthy organizations design their structures to reflect their functions, not the reverse! 'Form follows function'. They also maintain an active learning environment so as to learn continually. Appendix B includes a 'Health of the Organization Questionnaire' that allows the reader to assess their organization. This questionnaire can be used to measure the total health of a system, and to decide where to start in any change process.

Beckhard also provides us with a list of the characteristics of healthy organizations. They:

- have a strategic view
- energize others lower in the system
- create a structure that follows function
- make decisions at a point where the relevant information is held or 'comes together'
- have a reward system that balances what people know and what they do
- have relatively open communication
- reward collaboration, when it is in the organization's best interests
- manage conflict, don't suppress it
- view the organization as an open system and manage the demands put on it
- value difference
- actively learn, through feedback.

This may act as a useful checklist for assessing your own organization, noting its strengths and weaknesses.

But if healthy organizations need good, competent managers, how do general managers within the NHS rate?

What are Good Managers in the NHS?

A study of general managers by Johnson[6] is only briefly summarized here, so interested readers are referred to the full text. He identified two types of job competencies:

1. *Discriminating competencies*, which separate superior performers from average performers.
2. *Core competencies*: these were characteristics the sample had in common, which were needed to get the basic job done.

1. Discriminating competencies

- *Diagnosing and setting a direction for the organization*: has a broad vision of the future, 'a strategic view'; gets down to the key issues and making changes
- *Influencing*: identifies key people and uses force of argument to influence them
- *Political awareness*: considers the interests and motives of others; recognizes organizational constraints; keeps 'close to the ground' on current problems
- *Managing people*: uses and builds teams; informs and sets clear objectives
- *Handling conflict*: assesses others and deals with conflict to make progress on problems
- *Sensitivity*: considers others' feelings and makes time to listen
- *Determination to succeed*: has high personal energy; takes responsibility to make changes happen; takes on difficult issues

2. Core competencies

- Concerned to *improve service provision*; concerned about quality of care
- *Diagnoses and understands problems*
- *Evaluates own performance* in relation to specific outcomes

This book does not make the assumption that all general managers will be in the 'superior' category scale, nor that all organizations will score highly on 'healthiness', but it does accept reality. Examples gathered during the author's practice have been included to demonstrate how real issues can be tackled with real managers. They have been quoted anonymously with slight changes to avoid breaking confidence, but are designed to emphasize certain learning points that have been made theoretically.

I start by looking at the *present situation*, then the *desired future* – where do you want to get to? – and then, lastly, it follows the steps of transition to get to *where you want to get to* (see Figure 1).

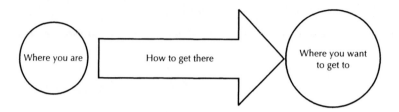

Figure 1

Structure of this Book

- Chapter 1 concerns the principals of complex change.
- Chapter 2 looks at the problems of creating change from within. It looks at leadership, and considers ways of getting systems into a state of readiness for change. Reader's exercises on promoting change are included, to work on a personal example.
- Chapter 3 looks at imposed change and the stress this causes in a system that is less ready for change. It also suggests ways of capitalizing on unplanned change. An in-depth case study demonstrates one way of taking advantage of external pressures to change.
- Chapter 4 looks at the different roles the nurse might take as a 'change agent'. This chapter includes a self-assessment tool which can help the reader to identify where to develop his or her managerial role. Evaluation is not commonly used in the author's experience, though one process of evaluation will be outlined which uses an accessible methodology. A reader's exercise demonstrates how to use this structured evaluation process.
- Chapter 5 is concerned with identifying the skills that individuals need to develop, so they can develop change in their organization.

References

1. Broome, A. K., *Health Psychology: Principals and Applications* (Chapman R. Hall, 1989).
2. Patient's Charter.
3. Pedler, M. J., Burgoyne and T. Boydell, *The Learning Company* (McGraw, 1991)
4. Kanter, R. M., *The Change Masters* (Allen & Unwin, 1984)
5. Beckhard, R., and R. T. Harris, *Organizational Transitions: Managing Complex Change* (Reading, Mass.: Addison-Wesley, 1987)
6. Johnson, J. E. A., *Job Competency Model* (NHS Training Authority Publication, 1987)

Chapter 1 Principles of Complex Change

This chapter views organizations as systems that deliver certain goods and services. Health services, however, don't exist in isolation: they affect and are affected by other organizations around them – for example, social services, local transport companies, drug companies, and so on. When making plans for possible changes, it is important not only to be specific about what the current system is, but also what our visions are, what we want it to be after the changes have been made, and how our stakeholders will be affected.

In order to plan for desirable changes, we will start by defining the present state and the processes that are involved in current service delivery.

The stages will be outlined briefly here so you can get a feel of the approach.

Defining the Present State

The purpose of an organization must be clearly defined in terms of its business, its reasons for existing, and the special and specific contribution it might make to a wider system. We can call this the 'mission' or 'purpose', within its wider environment. The first step in any change project is to be certain that there is agreement on the current purpose of the organization among the most significant people. It should be possible to describe the core purpose in one sentence. For instance, in a car factory, the core purpose might be: 'To produce cars of a high quality, while maximizing profits.' A secondary purpose might be: 'To provide a healthy working environment for employees.' In the NHS, a recovery unit might exist: 'To provide the highest quality of aftercare from operations to the largest number of patients, while maintaining appropriate professional standards, at the cheapest unit cost.'

The definition of core purpose might be – to look at where this organization adds value – its reason for being. For example, a GP fundholding practice might exist to provide accessible, humane, effective medical care to local people at the cheapest unit cost and the highest quality.

1. Identifying the system

Environmental mapping is a technique that can be used to gauge the total environment that affects, and is affected by, the system we want to change. The systems comprise the formal and informal structures, the goals, the cultural norms, the behaviour, skills and beliefs of individual members, and the interaction of all these (see Figure 2).

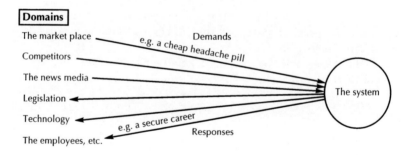

Figure 2 Domains for a drug company

One way of charting an organization's wider environment is to think of the organization as surrounded by a number of different, related systems, which might fall into sectors or 'domains'. For instance, typical domains for a drug company might be as shown in Figure 2. This is called an open system analysis: it looks at both the demands that are being placed on the system and the responses that it might choose to make. For instance, a primary care team might be obliged (for example, by legislation, such as the Children Act or the Children's Order in Northern Ireland) to attend to certain demands, but it may also have some choices to make. For example, it can decide whether to target its services to certain groups, such as those with high blood pressure, the over 80s or high-risk groups for HIV infection. Identifying the domains is the first step.

2. Demands

In clarifying the demands from the environment, it can help to imagine that the demand is being made verbally by a particular person or group of people. For instance, the public might be saying: 'The contract [or the Patient's Charter] says I will be offered an operation within twelve months.' The employees might be saying: 'We demand that we are consulted about any planned changes in the shift system.'

3. Responses

You can then imagine that the system is responding to these demands in a similar personalized way.

There is no reason to suppose that this mapping is static, since things change. So this scanning is not 'one off' – it needs to be done continually – and the map will usually be different as the demands and responses change.

Consider, for instance, one recent change most of us will have noticed. Applicants are now asked by insurance companies whether they have recently had their blood tested, to identify those at risk of HIV infection. This change has altered the insurance companies' *responses* to their clients, and the *demands* to them are now changing.

It may be tempting, as you begin to assess the current state, swiftly to assume that you know what changes are needed, and to impose them. It all becomes so obvious. But mostly change agents fail in their change attempts when they pay inadequate attention to diagnosis or analysis of all aspects of the situation. The need for a full diagnosis cannot be over-emphasized.

There are several diagnostic tools that are useful also in analyzing the future state, and one will be described here.

Describing the Desired Future State

Multiple scenario planning

In order to plan for change it is essential to have some idea of the future state you want, which gives something to aim for or to aspire to. But in these turbulent times multiple scenario planning is one way of coping with dynamic situations where we are unsure of the future and what it holds. A number of different scenarios can be taken into account, so that the plans can cover a number of different futures. For instance, over the next five years there might be a change in government, or an encouragement of private health insurance schemes for those on low incomes. Clever planning will manage to take account of many factors.

Beckhard suggests two steps in scenario planning (see Figure 3).

1. Agree on an ideal end state.
2. Select a midpoint and identify a specific date for this. Visualize the scenario and the actual conditions that will exist at that midpoint. The popular metaphor is to think of a helicopter ride and looking down to the midpoint, which is a few hundred feet below, describing what you would see that is different from 'now', using behavioural descriptions.

Diagnosis

Next, decisions need to be made on the following:

- What *types of changes* are needed? Are these changes in attitudes, behaviour, policies, practices?
- Which *systems* are involved? Which parts of the organization, and what are the boundaries/domains you will have to manage?
- Determine the system's *readiness for change*. What are the forces for and against change? How realistic is change? Is it attainable, and practical, or are you wasting your time?
- Determine *your own resources* in helping the change effort.

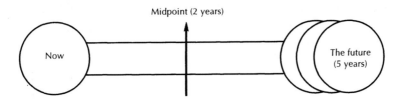

Figure 3 Scenario planning

What is your own motivation for change? Why do other people particularly want change? Is it because it may have career benefits? Because output will improve? Because short-term contracts will be renewed or improved? It is as well to be clear of your own driving forces and other people's motivation in helping you.

- The *level of energy that key people* bring to the effort. What is their readiness and capability to make change happen?
- *Which system is most vulnerable* to change? What is its linkage with other parts of the system? Can you use a domino effect, where, by starting in the right place, you can reduce the work by knocking down other blocks or constraints? For example, it may be easier and more economical to open up systems of communication that will then release shop-floor ideas than to work up one shop-floor scheme.

Changing behaviour

If changes in behaviour are needed, it may be useful to analyze the reasons for your staff's current performance. For instance, in an A&E Department, complaints had been made against staff at reception and the first contact nursing staff about their insensitive handling of ethnic minorities. The manager had identified this as a training problem, but he was encouraged to consider other possibilities before coming to this training solution. Indeed, there are many ways to approach such a performance problem.

Figure 4 is a systematic approach to performance problems.[1] Careful analysis of the reasons for the behaviour (or the performance deficit – the difference between how things are being

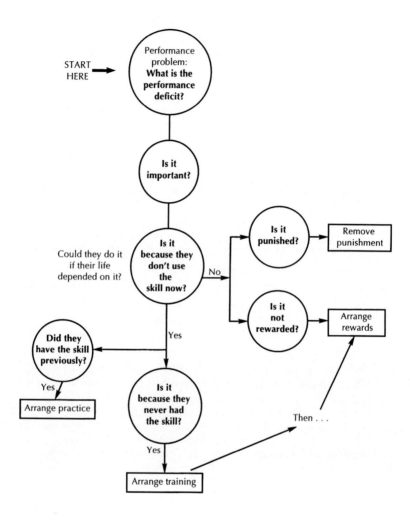

Figure 4 Changes wanted in behaviour

done and what you want) can pay off. This focuses your attention on two things:

1. the system (and the behaviours it is currently maintaining)
2. the person's reservoir of skilled behaviour (does the skill exist or is it just not being used?).

The A&E Department decided that the issue in question was important enough to address by asking: 'Do the staff have the interpersonal skills to be sensitive to patients?' They tested this by asking: 'Could they do it if their life depended on it?' If the answer is 'No', then the action is clear. It is necessary to train and develop the skill. If the answer is 'Yes', then it is clear that the skill once existed but has not been maintained.

It was decided in this case that it seemed more important to increase rewards for good, sensitive handling of all patients. On occasions, staff were seen being very sensitive, but only in dealing with certain categories of patients. The skill therefore existed, but probably was not being rewarded for *all* groups of patients. The solution was to arrange a case demonstration of good models which demonstrated social rewards for the staff in using sensitive skills towards the patients currently disadvantaged. Then an opportunity was made to elicit those particular skills in the group of staff using them less, and to structure the rewards for demonstrating such behaviours, in the problem setting, through the appraisal system.

In summary, the analysis in the A&E Department revealed that a more appropriate way to deal with the performance problem was to build in the department an informal social system that rewarded the behaviour, but also that a structured opportunity was needed to practise this behaviour and to build up formal rewards. Apparently this had been missing previously.

This example demonstrates that skills training is often not the only solution, since it is often the system that fails to maintain the skills. Full analysis of the current situation is often then needed to lead to the most economical plan for behaviour change.

Leverage

By now you will have identified the major domains involved in your problem, made plans for your future state, and identified key individuals' readiness, capability and domains which must be involved in order to have lasting effect. Your diagnosis can now proceed to *leverage*.

The change equation is popularly used to decide where to target your efforts. The equation says that change will occur if you can unsettle the *status quo* a little. This is done by creating a belief that things could be better, or by persuading key people that things are currently just not good enough. Also, if changes can be made simply and naturally, and the first steps are known, then this can help lever the *status quo*. The three major targets are therefore:

1. dissatisfaction with the *status quo*
2. a shared vision
3. knowledge of the first steps.

But the cost of change is always high. The change equation shows that three elements must be present to outweigh the cost of change:

$$(1) \times (2) \times (3) > (c) \qquad \text{where } (c) \text{ represents the cost of change}$$

This needs a little clarification, to show how to create unsettlement and some motivation for change. There are three entry points, all of which must be addressed.

1. Dissatisfaction with the status quo

This is a necessary part of change. It helps to create unsettlement. One way is to introduce ideas from outside, one of the recent introductions being *benchmarking*. Benchmarking is a simple notion of making comparisons between different organizations, and relating these measures to success. If certain units or organizations know that competing units are doing better than they are, then that might create dissatisfaction. But if a unit has tolerated a poor situation for a long time, it might continue to have a low aspiration and never strive for excellence. One general manager, when given some suggestions for improvements in his service, said: 'Isn't that rather too good for my hospital?' He was *too* satisfied with his current service! There was little aspiration.

It is sometimes necessary to cause *pain* in the system in order to generate some energy. However, energy can often be found in the system in people that are already hurting. These are a good source of energy for change.

2. A shared vision

In one particular hospital, senior people met very little. Even though individually these people didn't like the current situation and were critical of the service they were delivering, they had never got together as a group to agree on where they wanted to go. The fact that they all had very similar ideas was not obvious until they shared them. A shared vision can then give drive and encouragement to each other throughout the difficult change process.

3. Knowledge of the first steps

The incremental approach is an effective one, particularly when the first steps are broken down into clear simple actions. Many groups simply do not know how to take that first step, but once the first change is agreed, they find that energy is released. It all looks possible after all!

Change has both psychological and organizational costs, and there has to be enough time and support to lose old habits and to build up new ones. Throughout this change process, of course, old systems have to continue alongside the new ones. This will cause an increase in workload, so motivation has to be high in order to sustain staff over the difficult transition period, particularly if there are no additional resources.

Defining the Work to be Done

The characteristics of an effective change plan are that it must:

- link activities to the goals
- be specific
- be integrated, so the parts are connected
- be time-sequenced so there is a logical step-by-step series of stages – with dates!
- be adaptable, to take account of changes.

However, change will not happen unless a critical mass of significant people is brought together. *A critical mass is defined as the least number to make the change happen.* It is this group that will get commitment from the people in the organization, make the transition plan and turn the plan into action. Their readiness and capability needs assessing.

Key individuals can be charted to determine (a) who is *committed* to these particular changes and (b) who has *responsibility* that is relevant. It will be the job of the critical mass to develop commitment to the full and to decide what kind of management arrangements might be made for the transition state.

The Transition Plan

Special arrangements need to be made to drive the changes. The generally accepted options for managing transitions are as follows:

1. A head person in the organization becomes the project manager, or *a project manager is appointed.*
2. *A project team* is developed from the critical mass, or a *diagonal slice* is used to lead the project. A diagonal slice would take different levels of staff across different sections of the organization (see Figure 5). The aim here would be to shift to a more participative model, so a 'slice' of levels and roles across the organization increases general involvement. It may be beneficial to use natural leaders rather than representatives, although the entrepreneurial nurse or ambitious doctor who contributes well as an individual may fail to represent others and will have difficulty building commitment with them.

   In transition management, it can be useful to involve those managers who will have new roles in the future state. They will certainly have the most investment in getting it right and possibly in doing it the right way. When using a diagonal slice, avoid people who have direct line relationships to each other.
3. Beckhard uses the American expression 'a kitchen cabinet' to refer to colleagues, 'odd balls' or 'good old boys', in a network that an executive manager might consult on an

Section:	1	2	3	4	5	
					X	Manager
				X		Department head
			X			Supervisor
		X				Skilled worker
	X					Unskilled worker

Figure 5 Diagonal slice

informal basis. The phrase is derived from war-time meetings in President Roosevelt's kitchen, where his cronies dropped in for a chat and US policy was made! If these people are distant from any investment in the future state, then their opinions will tend to be more objective and might be more useful, but this will not build up commitment for the future state and future key players.

1. Transitions and the effects on people

Managers should never underestimate the powerful impact that change has on people. Consider for a moment the developments in recent years that have affected you personally: the rapid telecommunications and transport boom that has made the world seem a much smaller place, and changed work patterns from office to home; the changing technology that has speeded up international responsiveness to financial peaks and troughs; the changes in eating habits, fast food, health fads and the spread of Coca Cola to all corners of the globe! Each of these changes reflects large adjustments both in the organizations that have promoted them, and to consumers and those affected by the changes.

Many writers have suggested that managers have been *wise* to the mechanics of change, but have been *stupid* about the mechanics of transition! Change and transition are two very distinct processes. *Change* can be observed and planned. For example, we are able to see the trend to move particular groups of patients from mental hospitals into community houses, or

21

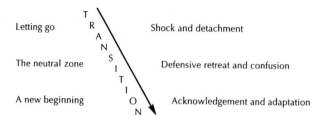

Figure 6 The stages of transition

for meals to be served that arrive plated rather than being cooked on the premises. Change can be planned, implemented and seen. In contrast, *transition* takes place as a three-part psychological process, where individuals (who, after all, are making the changes) are moving from one state to another, as shown in Figure 6. These stages can be anticipated and need to be planned.

1.1 Letting go of the old situation

Remember the last time you moved job or were promoted? I can recall counselling a recently promoted senior manager who felt overwhelmingly stressed. He was still trying to do his old job, going out on the wards ('I am just keeping in touch with the grass roots'), as well as taking on all the new managerial responsibilities, and learning the new office and administrative skills. It was stressing him to breaking point.

During counselling, it reassured him to be able to label the problem for himself, and to see the necessity of clarifying his new job responsibilities with his bosses and letting go of the old ones. He had to let go of the old role before he could begin the transition to the next.

Nurse managers are occasionally unable to 'let go' of all their technical expertise after they are promoted: 'I just can't keep up to date with it all." This leaves insufficient space to take on new demands and new skills. This is partly because of work overload, but can also arise due to a reluctance to leave the safety and competence of the old role for the risk taking or uncertainty of the new. Sometimes it is because of an unclear definition of the new role or a reluctance to delegate.

It may be useful here to outline the particular arenas of work that need different consideration as Health Service staff gain promotion or change job. A threefold classification of managerial activities might be useful here.[2]

1. *Technical* work is that part of the work relating to the profession, experience or qualifications. This is often the main work or tasks done before promotion to a managerial grade, and it is usually the main task of the unit or organization. For instance, a pathology lab will conduct tests (a technical task) while the head of department will manage its many activities. The closest a manager gets to the technical work is to ensure that the tests conform to certain criteria. However, on occasions, the manager may try his or her own hand at testing, but it is really the main function of the subordinates to perform these technical tasks.

2. *Administrative* work is concerned with organizational maintenance and routine procedures often defined by others, such as the superior or head of another department. In a ward or unit, this might be the filling in of activity returns, drawing up staffing shifts or checking expenses claims.

3. *Managerial* work involves setting priorities and precedents, and persuading others to action. It also involves checking what others have done, what they have promised to do, and dealing with day-to-day variations in demand and supply of services from that department. For instance, an A & E manager might have to swiftly reorganize the department layout and staff work pattern if major traffic accident victims are expected imminently; or a bed-booking manager might have complex negotiations if there is a steady and predictably high rate of 'failures to attend' for eye operations. These are managerial tasks.

In many organizations there is a confusion between these three activities, and a failure to recognize the particular and unique skills of the manager. It is also true to say that the most effective managers continue to keep in touch with the technical work, but do not allow themselves to get overwhelmed with updating their own technical expertise at the expense of developing and maintaining their administrative and managerial skills.

So, during a transition individuals have to let go of the old and build up their skills for the needs of the new role. But we need a way of identifying *all* those who will be affected by the changes, so each can manage his or her personal transitions. An example will illustrate.

Case study 1

In one older-style mental hospital, the upholsterer had not been involved in the far-reaching plans for change taking place in the hospital. The linchpin of this was the ward just above his workshop. He disliked the idea of patients having more freedom, and just above him!

One weekend, all the stored furniture was ruined when the patients (given more responsibility) decided to clean up their own area, wash the walls down and paint them. Water and paint simply ran down the walls into his workshop. When he arrived at work on Monday and saw the mess, it would have been a simple matter to have moved the furniture to save it being ruined, but he thought why should he? No one had asked his opinion and he had never liked these new ideas anyway. This proved that patients weren't fit to have more freedom anyway, didn't it?

His commitment to the plan was lacking. This example should highlight the need to identify *all* those affected by the change (the boundary domains), when making a transition plan.

One trick in identifying the essential boundaries is to try the 'planned neglect test'. This involves asking the question: 'If I don't bring these people, this department or this person on board and involve them in these changes, what will happen?' The answer may be 'Nothing', in which case you could plan to neglect the people, department or person. But this test will also help you to identify much more clearly which people will help or hinder.

The stage of 'letting go' of the old ways has been likened to the mourning process, and managers should expect the range of heightened emotions associated with this state – anger, denial, grief and helplessness – which need careful and effective management.

1.2 Going through the 'neutral zone' between the old and new reality

This is a time of confusion when new roles are unclear, and hope alternates with hopelessness and a loss of direction. Senior managers need to be aware of the stress at this time and to help people cope with the transition.

Being recruited internally is an example that can highlight the need for the neutral zone, because as a process it usually lacks the 'distance' between the two roles, which we see when someone moves for promotion. When a move is made to a new job, we often describe this as 'the honeymoon period' – a time to test and establish new norms, a time for enthusiasm and energy, before consolidating the role. When this is done internally, that distance and neutral zone is often lost, as illustrated in the following examples.

Case study 2

A colleague took up a post as general manager after having been more junior in the same unit. He made strenuous attempts to behave as differently as he could, throwing his colleagues and confidantes into confusion, adopting a different style of management 'by walkabout', opening his doors regularly one afternoon a week to speak to anybody from the shop-floor upwards, and refusing to undertake his old duties. He made an opportunity to create a neutral zone, a space to experiment and develop his new role. It also gave others a chance to relate to him differently.

Old, unresolved conflicts and dissatisfactions will often raise themselves again at these times, and even resignations will increase. Full preparation for this stressful time will certainly help acknowledge that uncertainty is a natural way to feel, and should even be predicted. Organizations that generally encourage innovation and change will not be immune to these effects, and they too can help by acknowledging it as an expected part of the change process. Then staff can work through it and start working on the building blocks of the next phase.

Case Study 3

A 'G' Grade theatre nurse applied for a business manager's post to work alongside the new Clinical Director in the Anaesthetic Department. She knew it would be difficult to release her 'hands on' role, but she felt she was ready to make the move, had studied hard, and had enjoyed the managerial aspects of her job.

When she heard that she had been successful, she spent some time thinking about how she could create a visible boundary between the old and the new persona. She decided to take a break between jobs, and took a two-week holiday. She came back with a different style of dress, and she agreed in private with the Clinical Director that she would be given clear management tasks very early on, for which she could be totally responsible. She managed to show from Day 1 that she intended to do different tasks and to do them differently.

1.3 A new beginning

This is the renewal stage where new skills are developed and people become accustomed to the new formal procedures, structures and systems. The process can be facilitated if plans are made to cope with the four major components (see Figure 7).

● *The informal organization*
In one ward, multidisciplinary communication was much improved and tribalism reduced when a new multidisciplinary rest room was allocated. Most members of staff in the outpatient department had always got on well socially, but replacing the nurses' rest room and the doctors' coffee room with one 'rest room' also increased formal communication.

● *The individual*
If individuals are to adapt to new demands they can benefit from clear and strong leadership. It helps if a leader and/or manager is seen to model new procedures and skills; for example, if a manager relates more sensitively to his or her subordinates, they are likely to relate more sensitively to *their* subordinates. Modelling can be a highly effective form of learning, particularly if the new behaviour is rewarded. This leader can also demonstrate how to manage and use conflict as a source of energy, rather than suppressing it. Encouraging the

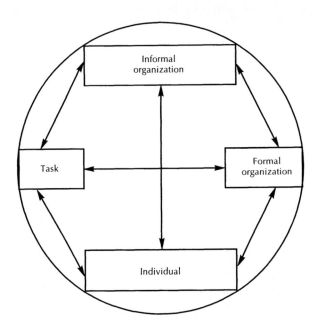

Figure 7 Transitions: the four organizational arenas to be addressed

emergence of conflict and using that energy is often one of the driving forces for this transition state.

● *The task*
Often, managers underestimate the need for additional resources during this transition period. New skills and relationships have to be learned and established, while old tasks usually have to be continued during the transition. Additional resources are nearly always needed, and even if only short-term resources are found, they help to provide a public acknowledgement of the additional load on people in making these changes.

● *The formal organization*
It is essential to design a clear and reasonable transition plan to make sure that the implementation or new beginning actually happens, and doesn't simply remain on paper. Structural

solutions were outlined earlier, and include the appointment of a transition manager or the strengthening of a natural leader's role during the transition period. The transition plan will need to concentrate on the following:

- goals to be achieved
- processes to get there
- a monitoring system to take care of the boundaries and to check on how the changes are affecting the total organization
- whether the processes of change are owned, or are the staff merely implementing someone else's plans? Who *owns* the change? (This is the essence of developing a *culture of change* rather than creating one change and leaving the system static afterwards.)
- how the changes will affect the leader, and his or her skills and future operation.

A case study might usefully demonstrate how, in reality, a transition plan might work.

Case study 4

An operating theatre manager, who had been recruited internally from his old post as nurse in charge of specialist theatres, was not keen to increase day case surgery. This had caused some frustration to the manager (who was worried about performance indicators), and was risking his future career. The conflict seemed to have a foundation in disagreements about roles and responsibilities that the general manager had been unable to explore with the previous operating theatre manager.

The initial diagnostic interview with the new theatre manager by an external consultant looked at:

- establishing what business he thought the department was in
- establishing the manager's role in this, as he perceived it (technical, administrative and managerial responsibility)
- outlining the demands for service and the influences on service delivery (both enabling and restraining)
- allowing an open-ended section to discuss any personal problems he might be having with these responsibilities and the transition to managing the service.

The diagnosis revealed his personal ambivalence about general management and the failure to acknowledge his own shift in role as he moved to theatre manager. He had been unable to create enough space from his previous role for other people to treat him differently, and this included his new boss.

It was also necessary to clarify the core purpose of the department *now*, and the theatre manager's role and responsibility in this. He felt his task was unclearly defined and his formal working relationships with clinicians and the general manager were unclear.

There was also a failure to manage his personal transition from a technical and administrative role to a managerial role, which was creating personal difficulties in relationships.

If we study carefully the components of transition (Figure 7), it helps to look into each arena – the informal, formal, individual and task components. In this case, the new theatre manager had maintained the same strong informal relationships, had unclear formal relationships and individual responsibilities, and the tasks therefore were not developing in the way they should. He had developed a high level of informal involvement, dealing with local squabbles and creating very cohesive and effective teamwork, but this still took up much of his time, and by failing to increase the responsibilities of the operating team leaders, he retained the kind of grassroots trouble-shooting role he had previously taken as nurse manager. He was unable to get enough time and space to take on his new managerial role. It was becoming clear that he needed to deal with the formal organization by clarifying the new demands, managing his boundaries (with clinicians) and working up the roles of his subordinates to respond to these demands.

The solutions to this problem were complex. Some lay in developing a proper transition plan, both personally for the manager's career development, and organizationally for the whole theatre directorate and its boundaries. The theatre manager began to accept the concept of a *managed unit* rather than an *administered unit*. He also planned to develop a higher level of managerial skill.

2. Stress

It is probably already clear to the reader, through these examples, how stressful such change processes are, and how difficult it often is to provide the necessary support and help to those going through the transition process. Although it is not a central focus of this particular book, it is probably useful here to briefly outline a way of looking at stress, and to be aware of some specific tools for identifying the components of stress, so that the transition period can be approached in a productive, rather than a destructive way.

Milne and Watkins,[3] in an interesting study of the stressful effects of the shift system for nurses, demonstrated that staff did not find rotation shifts a particular strain, but this was only because they increased their coping strategies to deal with it. It is generally assumed that if we increase stress, then there is an increase in strain. These authors usefully separate these two factors, and suggest that there are many ways in which nurses can help their own adjustment to stress by increasing problem-solving skills, relabelling stressors and developing more realistic expectations. Indeed, they feel that this sort of training should become part of the management process, to help staff through the change process. Managers can also help by giving personal support, by increasing training in coping and by improving work conditions. All these activities come well within the remit of the manager's responsibility. So, the three interacting components are:

- stress
- coping
- strain

In other words, there are plenty of *stressors* in the work environment, but the individual can reduce the *strain* of these by increasing his or her own *coping* mechanisms. This will modify the effects of *stress*. Any readers wishing to explore this area of literature further or to improve their skills at identifying stress, coping or strain in their own workforce may find the following tools useful.

- *Occupational Stress Indicator,* developed by Cary Cooper[4]: this is a scale for managers and measures the causes and effects of occupational stress.
- *The General Health Questionnaire*: Banks *et al.*[5] review the use of the shorter twelve-item scale for mental health screening in occupational settings.
- *The Nursing Stress Scale* developed by Grey-Toft and Anderson[6] rates the frequency of stressful events in the nurse setting.
- *The Coping Responses Questionnaire,* developed by Billings and Moos,[7] looks at three aspects – active cognitive, active coping and avoidance.

For more general reading in the area, Matteson and Ivancevich[8] have written a readable book on work stress.

Readiness to Change

In assessing readiness to change, we need to look at both the individual's state and the organization's state. Also, individuals will be more ready to change if change is a usual part of that organization's life.

Let us simply consider the major types of change we are asking an individual to make, then the stages of planning a successful transition may become clearer. We may want change in the *tasks* performed, the *formal* structure and also the way we relate *informally* to each other (see Figure 7).

Case study 5

A specialist GU clinic moving to new premises took the opportunity to expand the medical staff and to change the working practices, by developing a Nurse Practitioner role for the clinic's nursing staff.

Tasks were changed in that nurses extended their role, by taking on new skills, new training, having different responsibilities and having to relate to different medical staff with different practices.

New policies had to be developed and monitored; the formal structure therefore changed.

Informally, new contacts and friendships had to be established as the tasks had altered shifts and the way people were grouped.

The success of such changes will depend on the level of security felt by both the individual and the system. The individual in transition is probably the area we have covered least, although we have already recognized the stressful effects of transition and how to recognize strain on individuals in the system. However, the forces in the individual (see Figure 8) and the forces in the system combine to provide an overall level of security. It is this which will determine whether changes are likely to be made and how costly they might be.

1. The individual

In Figure 8 we can see that the individual's range of skills and personal confidence, ability to tolerate ambiguity and change, and level of motivation will all have an effect on

31

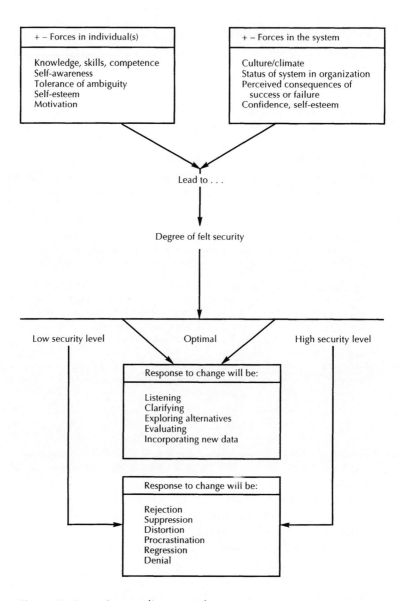

Figure 8 Assessing readiness to change

their potential for change. Indeed, the transition state is often characterized as being high in uncertainty, stress, energy and increased conflict. It is the individual's own state and self-confidence that will allow him or her to take on, or reject, the new uncertain demands being placed on them.

2. The system

Similarly, the climate of the organization, and whether it is generally concerned with change, will affect responsiveness to change. If it respects and supports the idea of uncertainty, and views the outcomes as important, then this will affect the degree of felt security. The ability to tolerate ambiguity and uncertainty at this stage is essential if change is to happen.

There are special needs during this transition state.

- There should be a clear image of the future.
- There should be transition plans that consider the four major domains (Figure 7) – the task, the formal and informal systems, and the individual.
- Leadership should be proactive and visible; it provides an opportunity (through role modelling) for leaders to demonstrate how to deal with uncertainty and conflict.
- Conflict needs to be redirected and managed, and not suppressed. If suppressed, the process will be losing energy, which could have been used to fuel and drive the transition process.
- Areas of uncertainty should be acknowledged as natural to the process of change. But high levels of uncertainty should be avoided. This can be done by pacing the plans, sharing the broad outlines of the plans and creating information systems that can give feedback on progress.

It may be useful at this stage to consider the transition as a learning process for the whole organization. For organizational learning to occur, there has to be some kind of need or desire for change. Consider the change equation given earlier which suggested that you can 'lever' the situation, either through creating dissatisfaction with the current state or increasing aspiration for the future, so that a disequilibrium was encouraged. The process of creating a desire for change can be

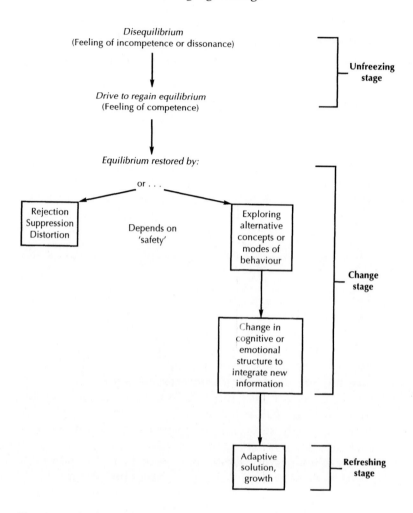

Figure 9 The learning process

described as the unfreezing stage (see Figure 9). This unfreezing stage is a state of *dissonance,* of conflict, or lack of direction. If we use a physical sciences parallel, dissonance can be
defined as: 'a state that drives the system or individual to
regain some kind of equilibrium.' There is a need to gain control over imbalance or uncertainty, and to try to restore some
kind of order. Equilibrium can be restored by making changes,

but people can equally well reject, suppress and distort changes so that the old ways are valued again, and change does not occur.

The *freezing stage* follows on from the change state, and is a stage where solutions are found and changes are consolidated.

Summary

Unless there is a climate of innovation and change, the tendency is for organizations to remain the same. But by using diagnostic and leverage techniques, we can irritate and begin the wish to change. If it is well planned and driven, then it is less likely to cause a retreat or regression back to the old state. Change is an active process which has to be levered, nurtured and rewarded. An organization that is used to change, and is fit for it, can cope with the high level of stress and strain that goes with change, is more likely to adapt and grow than one which has no culture of change.

References

1. Mager, R. F. and P. Pipe, *Analysing Performace Problems* (Belmont, Calif.: Fearon Publishers Inc., 1970).
2. Torrington, D. P. and J. B. Weightman, 'Technical Atrophy in Middle Management', *Journal of General Management* (1982) **8**(4), 422–31.
3. Milne, D. and F. Watkins, 'An Evaluation of the Effects of Shift Rotation on Nurses Stress, Coping and Strain', *International Journal of Nursing Studies* (1986) **23**(2), 139–46.
4. Cooper, C., *Occupational Stress Indicator* (NFER, 1988).
5. Banks, M. H. *et al.*, 'The Use of the GHQ as an Indicator of Mental Health in Occupational Studies', *J. Occ. Psychol.* (1980) **53**, 187–94.
6. Grey-Toft, P. and J. G. Anderson, 'The Nursing Stress Scale Development of an Instrument', *J. Behav. Assessment* (1981) **3**, 11–23.
7. Billings, A. G., and R. H. Moos, 'The Role of Coping Responses and Social Resources in Attenuating The Stress of Life Events', *J. Behav. Med.* (1981) **4**, 139–57.
8. Matteson, M. T., and J. M. Ivancevich, *Controlling Work Stress* (Jossey-Bass, 1987).

Chapter 2   Leadership and Creating Change from Within

This chapter concentrates on initiating change from within by looking at leadership and its role in maintaining a renewing organization and the role of teamwork. It concludes with reader's exercises on evaluation and creating change from within.

Leadership

Research on leadership shows that there is certainly not just one style of leadership that will be successful at all times.

'There is no such thing as an effective leader in all situations.'
(Margerison, 1979)

Without going into too much detail about this research, it is essential here to realize that, because 75 per cent of a manager's time is generally spent talking with people, and indeed people are the basic resource of the NHS, managing people is the essence of nursing management. Of course, a wide range of these leadership skills can be learned, but such skills are not always needed continually; they are best used selectively to match different situations. (For more information, see the volume *Managing People* in this series.[1])

The group analysis tool, which can be found more extensively in Belbin,[2] demonstrates that people can develop more than one role, and use the one most relevant to the task and the makeup of the rest of the group. So too, leaders need a variety of operating styles (see p. 115), and it is the matching of the style to the situation that becomes a major leadership skill.

Mintzberg[3] suggested the following range of group roles that leaders may adopt.

- Figure-head role: the ceremonial public speaking role
- Group leader role: resolving operational problems
- Liaison role: being a representative of your group
- Information role
- Spokesperson role: representing your profession externally
- Entrepreneurial role: innovating and encouraging change
- Resource allocator: deciding who does what
- Disturbance handler: dealing with conflict
- Negotiator and conciliator

Michael Walton,[4] in his book *Management and Managing*, gives a series of exercises that help managers profile their own pattern of leadership skills and leadership roles. Readers might like to assess themselves, using these methods.

For the purposes of managing change, creating a culture of change and innovation is undoubtedly relevant to leadership issues. Burns[5] suggests two leadership styles:

1. transformational
2. transactional

These are distinguished by the characteristics shown in Table 1.

Turrell[6] has suggested that organizational change is led by *transformational* leadership, a style that works on ideas and visions, and builds common commitment. *Transactional* managers are more conforming, explicit and orderly in achieving their tasks. Turrell suggests that the orderly breaking down of the tasks by transactional managers often leads to a loss of vision and energy, whereas the transformational leader can keep a distance, a strategic or a helicopter view of the whole.

- The transformational leader is more effective at large visionary changes of a new or renewing organization
- The transactional leader is best at the systematic work of a leader at the consolidation stage

Table 1 Leadership styles

Transformational	Transactional
Empowers	Bargains
Inspires by vision, ideals	Is task centred
Mixes home and work	Separates home and work
Has a long-term focus	Has a short-term/medium-term focus
Challenges	Coaches sheltered learning
Rewards informally, personally	Rewards formally
Is emotional, turbulent	Is comfortable, orderly
Simplifies	Complicates

1. What is the leader's role in change?

It is often suggested that less management and more leadership is needed in the NHS to cope with the increasing complexity of services and the world surrounding the service. The NHS could be viewed (with the rapid changes imposed on it over the last fifteen to twenty years) as a massive change project, which has created an increasing demand for leadership skills.

Benis et al.[7] suggest that good leaders should create:

- a clear vision of the future
- a culture of change
- dynamic management of the boundaries
- an organization as a learning community, where approaches change and are actively developed, in tune with the emerging issues.

Adair[8] highlights a leader's three main responsibilities (see Figure 10). This style of leadership is more reflective of the transactional leadership role, as described by Burns. Even though Adair suggests that the following list is not definitive (since the sheer variety of managerial tasks and situations is so great for a manager), these general functions are usually demanded of a leader manager:

- planning
- initiating
- controlling
- supporting

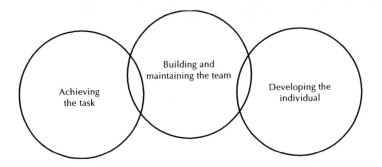

Figure 10 Leader's three main responsibilities

- informing
- evaluating

These particular leadership skills reflect the task-orientated trans-actional leader, but Benis' work would suggest that transactional leaders may be less proficient at leading significant, revolutionary change.

2. Leadership and teamwork

For a fuller discussion of the literature relating personality traits, styles and situations to leadership in nursing, readers are referred to Lancaster and Lancaster.[9] These authors re-emphasize the need for leadership skills to match the demands of each situation, so *matching* becomes one of the skills of a good leader. More recently, emphasis has been placed on lead-ership skills in understanding, motivating and managing a team or group. To help a group function well, the leader needs to take account of the task in hand, and the skills and styles of the individual group members. Indeed, research claims a strong relationship between the productivity of groups and the feelings of fulfilment and contribution of each individual member.

It is important to recognize the shifting balance between the leader and each team member, and the extent to which each individual is invited to contribute to the process. It may be useful for readers to consider their current practices. For example, a nurse may be given prescribed activities by the ward manager (*TELLS*), but may take part in ward meetings where the doctor in charge wants to hear his or her opinion of the patient's state (*CONSULTS* or *PARTICIPATES*).

Plant[10] has likened a manager's role to a conductor and the individual team members to players in an orchestra. This highlights the unique role of each player, but also emphasises the combined (or *CORPORATE*) responsibilities. A conductor has her own realm of skill and managerial responsibility in helping an orchestra play together, but she also respects the realm of skill of each of the players. What the orchestra plays is the leader's decision. Whether the tune played is a good one depends on co-operation, and a clear understanding of the unique contributions of each player and the limits of responsibility of each. So a good manager will decide the tune to be played, but only after ensuring that the orchestra is energized and competent, prepared to co-operate and knows its own limits. The leader will take account of the team members' competence and motivation in deciding just how much delegation is possible.

The Role of Leadership in Initiating Change

One of the paradoxes of the transformational leader is encapsulated in the phrase 'No pain, no gain'. So, when a leader creates a dynamic environment, he or she is likely to become associated with the pain of disruption and dissonance. The leader must have the ability 'to empower others to endure the costs of change',[11] otherwise the pain will be too much for the workforce. For instance, one general manager is aware of his public image as 'the butterfly' with 'high score on ideas, but low on follow-through', but his senior staff thrive on the excitement and his dynamism.

In the NHS currently we all too often hear people saying: 'We need time to settle down, we've had enough changes, we need time to consolidate.' It is true that there are increasing pressures, such as delivering cost improvements, for competitive tendering, and to move services for chronic problems into the community. However, there are also pressures from within.

Consider again the example of the butterfly manager. He is internally driven, a transformational manager who creates uncertainty and change around him, but he has enough strengths and skill to maintain a learning environment. He can still create high motivation in others, even though they know that not all of his schemes will stay the course. As a conductor, he encourages experiment; he wants to try new tunes! Not all those he's attracted to are performed or even finished. He sees his general manager role mainly as a change agent. Indeed, in the American book *The Nurse as a Change Agent*, by Lancaster and Lancaster, the nurse manager's main role is defined as a change agent.

Creating a Climate of Change

Successful organizations in the market place have to adapt continually to a swiftly moving economy. For them, the power to self-generate is often the key to survival and success, but to do this they need a strong culture of learning, taking risks, making mistakes, and learning from them. Yet, paradoxically, they still have to deliver the usual goods. There are more dilemmas and paradoxes inherent in these types of renewing organizations which could usefully be outlined here, so readers can identify the tensions in their own organization.

1. Loose–tight

An example of this paradox is the fostering of divergent, original and even contradictory ideas (loose) at the same time as working efficiently (tight) to short-term goals. A functioning organization needs to be alert and ready with new ideas, so it can respond to the variety of demands and opportunities the environment might make, and yet still keep on making the products. The bureaucratic, compartmentalized structures of an organization like the NHS often serve to stifle such innovation. One way to remain responsive is to allow a high level of delegation, which can help the organization to maintain control, but can delegate authority for ideas to flourish within specific boundaries or limits. For instance, one Trust gives such tight limits (in policy-making and negotiating its boundaries, in recruitment and in budgetary controls) that the general managers were offered *only* 'tight' not 'loose' control. The level of innovation was very small. The good manager has to offer freedoms, but with boundaries.

2. Technical and/or managerial role

Good leaders and managers will maintain some links with their technical base, but develop additional management skills. In Chapter 1, we saw the tensions that can exist when an individual is promoted from a technical or administrative job to the managerial level. Some organizations assist individuals through these transitions, by helping them integrate the technical and managerial aspects into the one role, but the good manager clearly releases their hold on technical knowledge.

3. Continuity

In a bureaucracy, managers, as individuals, are seen as replaceable, but this mobility of individuals is antagonistic to the views expressed here on the importance of key individuals in the change effort. A certain continuity of the critical mass is essential, not only to mobilize the change effort, but also to acknowledge, note achievements and keep a momentum of progress. It is hard work developing any changes, and if key people are changed, then these processes will need to be renegotiated and re-established with other key individuals, which can lead to a loss of energy. Nevertheless, short-term contracts are becoming a way of life, and our methods need to take account of changing key personnel.

4. Strategy vs. operation

During crises, top management have to grasp control and attend to the immediate concerns. In the NHS, we have seen wards closing and the freezing of posts, in response to sudden financial pressures. There is a natural tension between short-term and long-term actions. It cannot be denied that we have to grasp the tiller when crises occur, but long-term development issues have to run alongside these short-term operations and crises, and sometimes these different aspects of the work are incompatible, or antagonistic.

Successful commercial and public organizations recognize the need to take quick, centralized decisions simply to survive and ride a crisis, while at the same time recognizing the need to build up staff capacity at all levels, so keeping the ability to innovate and to renew, and maintain responsiveness to the market place. It is this which will ensure their long-term survival.

In strategic planning exercises with top management we find confusion and tension between the 'tasky' work (how to save £1m. by Monday), and the long-term strategic work (how to improve care to the over-80s). These are the in-built tensions of time scale that most organizations have to balance. It may become clearer after reading the following sections on developing teamwork how different team methods might be needed to work on these different types of tasks, which have different time spans, and different levels of certainty and problem solving. For instance, working on a *strategic issue* (how to develop services to the over-80s or more priority for care in the community) needs the support and commitment of a responsible management team and other key individuals, but the same people are not relevant for an *operational task* (such as developing a kitchen for cook–chill meals), which needs different key people and is a more *certain* task.

If the climate of the organization is one of change and self-generation, and is more of a learning community, then uncertainty is more easily dealt with, and the ideas will keep coming. If the culture encourages challenge and review, and there is a close contact with the changing demands on the organization, then short-term crises and sudden operational challenges will be dealt with appropriately and constructively. The solutions are also likely to be congruent with the vision that has been built up for the organization's long-term future. But there will usually be tension. This is between the steady building up of long-term plans and the sudden operational crises that can dominate the 'here and now'.

Developing Teamwork

Intrinsic to the discussion on creating a renewing system, a change culture, is the importance of getting commitment and involvement of groups of people in the organization, and using their energy and expertize to generate and sustain change. One of the essential ingredients in maintaining this type of renewing organization is the building up of a common vision and working together towards common goals.

The various ways of improving and using teamwork will not be detailed in full here, but it may be useful to direct those wanting to investigate this area in more depth to a very practical manual by Gawlinski and Graessle.[12] The authors suggest analyses, exercises and processes that readers might like to use; for example, mapping relationships, active listening and negotiating, managing meetings and giving feedback. They also set up tasks for readers which help teams develop a common purpose, agree a vision and share values.

However, teamwork should be designed selectively. The indiscriminate use of teams has received some balanced criticism from Critchley and Casey.[13] These authors suggest that different types of problems are best dealt with by different types of teams. First, they acknowledge that the capacity for good teamwork is important in healthy organizations. They list the characteristics of a functioning team.

- People care for each other.
- People are open and truthful.
- Decisions are made by consensus.
- There is strong team commitment.
- Conflict is dealt with and feelings are expressed.

Second, Critchley and Casey identify further critical variables, which have become obvious to them through their team-building efforts in industry and with public services. They suggest that teamwork is more appropriate for tasks where there is a *high degree of uncertainty* (for instance, in strategic issues), and a greater need to share the process together and to come to a common solution. Here, teamwork is appropriate. If the task has *very little uncertainty*, and is a relatively technical task (changing a kitchen to cook–chill meals), then teamwork is a luxury and is not appropriate, since it is really only necessary to involve those people who have the necessary technical expertise.

Third, they suggest that teams that have to deal with such high levels of uncertainty are *stressful* (and attempts will often be made to avoid the process, because of that). It therefore takes a particularly high level of interpersonal skills to successfully motivate and operate teams for the tasks with high levels of uncertainty.

In summary, leadership issues are complex. There is no such thing as a born leader, although certain characteristics may help (like intelligence) and certain skills are desirable. Rather, it is the ability to select and apply skills, according to the needs of each situation, that makes good leaders. The leadership style that is most likely to promote rapid change is suggested to be the *transformational* leader; that is, someone who creates visions, ambiguity, uncertainty and turbulence.

However, the particular role taken by a leader in groups and the ability to develop complementary roles in that group will determine the team's effectiveness, rather than one particular skill. For each management issue, it is wise to be clear about the nature of the task, and the role and purpose of the team addressing the issue. It is certain that different skills will be needed to fit the different issues that complex organizations need to address. So, the ability to diagnose each problem and to set up appropriate processes to address them is most important, particularly in judging its level of uncertainty.

Creating Change from Within

Open systems theory views organizations as a complex of subsystems, which affect each other to a greater or lesser extent. It makes the case for full diagnosis, to include affected parts.

For example: the efficiency of the supplies department affects the care given in the operating theatres; the personnel department affects the swift replacement of staff and therefore the continuity of service in the records department; the communication skills of the reception staff affect the way the patients view the hospital at first outpatient appointment.

Surrounding (or boundary) services can also affect the delivery of the target organization or system. For instance, Social Services policies can alter the criteria clinical staff may use for discharging an elderly person from a medical ward on a Friday; or local phone lines or self-help groups can affect the number of people self-referring to alcohol-treatment services or genito-urinary medicine clinics, and the problems they are concerned about.

Probably more examples are not needed to highlight the interacting nature of systems, subsystems and their boundaries. But it may help to remind readers of the possible knock-on effect that one part of a system will have on another, when changes are made. It is therefore essential that these related systems are clarified at the diagnostic stage, to include them as part of the planned changes.

1. Diagnosis

Within each part of a system, there are internal relationships of peoples, structures, technologies, tasks, goals, cultures and processes (see Figure 11). In any diagnostic process, these relationships always need attention, whether the target for diagnosis is only a small part of the hospital (for example, the records department) or the whole organization, like an acute hospital Trust.

Each part of the larger 'whole' (the target system and its boundaries) will, of course, have missions or reasons for operating, which will relate to the target system. Hence, the term 'open systems' suggests that no system can be understood or changed without attention to its wider environment, which must become part of the total view. It is within these complex surroundings that *demands* are made on the system, and it is to this environment that the system offers its *responses*. The following case study is intended to highlight the need to focus on the subsystems and their interrelationship, when planning changes.

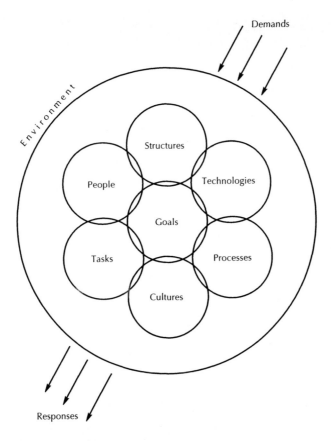

Figure 11 The organization as an open system

Case study 6

In working with a psychology department it became clear that this department was acting in some isolation. It needed a new way of thinking so that is related to the wider environment in which it was operating, and could survive by developing relevant contracts and services.

The work with the psychologists started with a diagnostic phase, identifying the department's range of choices of response to the range of demands that were made on it. It became clear that the department needed to clarify, agree and then communicate its

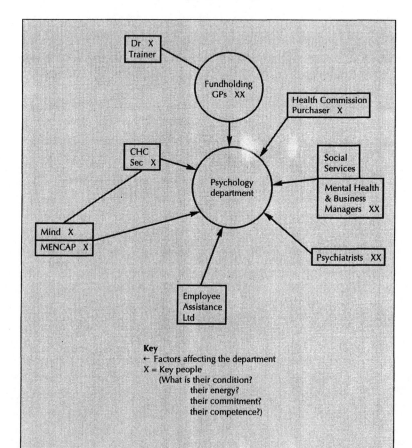

Figure 12 Mapping the environment

mission (its purpose, its business). It needed some clear agreement between members of the department on where it was going. Until these things were done, boundaries could not be managed.

Boundary management had been given little priority in the past. As a result, there were continual hassles from the psychiatrists in particular and from the Business managers who felt the psychology department was not fitting into the overall mission of the unit. It was therefore deemed useful to 'map' the environment, listing all the interrelated systems and grouping them into 'domains', noting the key people and their condition. Figure 12 shows the 'map' they developed.

It was interesting to watch the psychologists' realization that useful or capable key people had not been involved and that much time had been spent on other key people who didn't have the energy or commitment to help or support any changes. A second map was therefore made, to summarise the potential for change. This was done using the 'planned neglect' technique, asking questions like: 'What if we ignore this domain or if we ignore this person?' This approach sorts out those people or domains that are important to work with. To be economical, it is essential to only deal with those that can or will have some effect – and this planned neglect technique sorts out the key players and systems.

Next, they began to define the changes required, by taking a helicopter view of the future. What would the department like to be doing differently? What would the new system look like? The psychologists felt that much more of the demands for training and staff development of other staff should be met, and less response made to the demands for individual therapy, which could ultimately be met by counselling staff, if they were fully trained and supervised. Thus, the 'changed service' would look (to a helicopter pilot) different. Psychologists would be working more on training, research and development, and the consultancy process and doing less one-to-one therapy.

It is not difficult to see the implications of such proposals – the reduction of clinic sessions, the integration into others' programmes, and so on. So, the next stage was to more closely define the exact changes needed, in terms of:

● attitudes
● behaviour
● policies
● practices.

Once this was done, it was possible to analyse the parts of the system (domains) involved in making these changes, and to find the people with the energy to help these changes happen. The group undertook a more detailed analysis of readiness and capability of these key people and domains.

As the process proceeded, it became even clearer that different psychologists had different views about what they should be there for. Because this had not been clarified, it was difficult for the head of department to be a negotiator and ambassador, and to market the department's services on behalf of the others.

The reasons for their main purchaser's unease were now also clearer. How could they contract if it was unclear about the business it was in? It became clear than an agreed vision about the future was a first priority. Once this was done, the staff could move on to restructuring and setting up a system that related better to its functions. In the most acceptable organizational development language, 'form was to follow function'!

In summary, the department had to negotiate with its surrounding systems to agree on the main service it should provide (the demands). Then they had to decide how to prioritize and deliver their service. The internal structure they adopted had to alter, so it was the most effective in delivering the new service. It is easier to make this kind of change in a dynamic culture where individuals *expect* to change their contribution as the demands change and where their own technology develops.

1.1 Mission

All organizations need to be clear, at any moment in time, what their 'business' is, so it may be useful to clarify what we mean by the mission of an organization.

Mission is the reason to be, the identity of the organization, system or department. A mission statement usually lists two or three priorities. It is different from goals or objectives, which are more to do with 'where you want to get to'. It should say something about the values and beliefs behind the statement. For example, it may be 'to deliver family planning advice and clinical services in an acceptable, accessible and equal way to a local population'. Alternatively, it may be couched in value terms – 'that each contributing individual or employee is valued for him or herself' (giving an expectation that a unique contribution is as appropriate from a catering assistant as it is from a consultant). Another mission statement might include 'to develop a dynamic culture, where the process of change becomes expected' (here players would expect to be part of a dynamic, renewing system).

Such mission statements can usually be contained in three sentences or less, with priority being given in the order of the statements. They provide a back-check for each stage of your change programmes, to ensure you are still working within your organization's agreed mission.

Readers may be wondering how they can proceed from having a clear mission or business to setting about creating the changes and achieving the vision – moving from now → to then. Exercises are fully described at the end of the chapter which will take you through the process, in the following steps:

- diagnosis
- the vision
- building commitment.

But before trying the exercises (pp. 55–8), you are asked to consider the issue of *evaluation*, which could be built into your change programme right from the beginning, not as an afterthought. It gives structure to your efforts. Unfortunately, few organizations devote much time and energy to evaluation. It is not seen as adding all that much value.

Evaluation – Is it Working?

In this context, evaluation can be described as a systematic gathering and interpretation of information to aid decision making. It is concerned with both *outcomes* (for example, did patients get discharged quicker?) and *the process* or means of getting there (for example, training all direct care staff in interpersonal skills).

There are two types of evaluation of particular relevance to the management of change:

1. *Formative evaluation:* this is generally used to help improve the programme as you go along;
2. *Summative evaluation:* this type of evaluation is often done by outsiders. It provides a summary statement of the programme's effectiveness – for instance, how well it achieved preset goals. It is usually undertaken after the programme is complete, and can be used to shape up future programmes. It lacks the interactive *action* element of the formative approach.

We are only concerned here with formative evaluation.

1. Setting objectives

The starting point of any change project and for formative evaluation involves the setting of objectives. These need to be operationally defined so that two different observers agree on what is to be changed and the means of achieving that change. Consider the objective 'to reduce the waiting list by 20 per cent'. Astute readers will notice problems with this. There is no time span and so two observers might have quite different understandings of what is a waiting list. One might take the view that it consists of all those people who have seen the consultant once and are waiting for treatment; another might view it as all those people who are still waiting for their first consultant appointment. You can envisage the ensuing difficulties if this is not cleared up at the outset, and if operational definitions are not agreed about these measures. If this is not done, the results will be interpreted in different ways, and it is not easy to judge if the programme is being successful.

2. Goals

These are the general statements that usually outline the purpose of the intervention or programme – for example, to improve patient satisfaction. They are less specific than the objectives.

3. Soft systems methodology

Remembering that evaluation of complex change involves an outline of our proposed intentions (goals), the outcomes we can expect (outcomes) and how we get there (procedures, processes), one of the most useful methods of evaluating organizational change has been the soft systems approach.[14] This approach allows us to redefine the systems involved, as the programme develops. It builds a conceptual model of the whole system involved in the change. The definition of the system tends to change as the work proceeds.

This constant review is part and parcel of any change process. However, some managers are impatient – because on occasions the objectives seem clear. They therefore believe that they know what to do to put it right, and simply want to get on with the process. But inadequate diagnosis is the most common cause of failure in change projects. In such a situation, managers may later say: 'We don't seem to be getting there, details and trivia keep impinging.' But what is often seen as trivia or detail could, in a thorough diagnosis, be interpreted as central to the overall change process and its success, and should have been addressed earlier. An example might help to illustrate the point.

Case study 7

The Business Manager of a mental health Trust wanted to speed up the move into the community. She had timed and costed the programme and wanted to get on. But we encouraged her to invest more time in diagnosis and build up commitment for change among the key people in her organization. She later agreed that because of this she noted problems in advance, and her change had a greater likelihood of success. She mapped the Community Mental Health Trust in its total environment and consequently felt it necessary to deal with a much wider complex of interconnected systems. For instance, the unions were edgy about security of employment for auxiliary and nursing staff. They needed to know what the changes meant and how it would affect their members, before they were fully committed to being involved in the transition. In addition, the housing department had had little involvement in meshing their planned development into plans for rehousing mentally ill patients, and the medical staff had been planning to run outpatient clinics in the mental health centres. The philosophy of care that the centre staff had agreed on was at variance with this, and negotiations were needed to bring these groups into some common understanding of the purpose or mission of these mental health services. Thus, what originally might have appeared to be 'detail' to the Business Manager in fact turned out to reflect quite basic issues and domains that needed to be included and resolved.

This example is given at some length to demonstrate how defining and redefining the total system is essential. As changes are made, they often start to affect parts of the system that were not originally seen as central to success.

This rigour in identifying the systems involved can help the planning process, as well as the change agent, who might miss something in what appears to be an unrelated system and which may later hinder the changes.

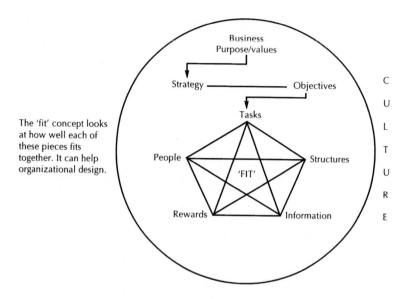

Figure 13 The concept of 'fit' (loosely based on Jay Galbraith)

Once the systems have been defined, it can be useful to use a simple evaluation system that concentrates on identifying the exact *inputs* and *outputs* you are expecting from individuals or parts of the system.

The concept of 'fit' may be useful here (see Figure 13 as developed by Jay Galbraith). It shows the internal elements that are involved in any organization delivering services or goods. It may be that certain areas are more problematic than others. For instance: do the formal structures make the tasks easier or difficult? Is the system of ordering from stores so complex that ward staff prefer to 'borrow' from neighbouring wards when they need something urgently? Each area needs addressing for effective performance.

Evaluation is not something you should do at the end of the programme. It is something you plan in right from the beginning, in line with your intentions. It helps you get it right!

Soft systems methodology[15] is a methodology that has been developed to look at the complex systems involved in organizational change. Checkland[16] suggests that it isn't possible to specify the finite systems involved right from the beginning, but it is essential to keep respecifying as the view changes. Thus, the methodology is entirely suited to organizational change, where we often need to change tack and to reassess the new systems involved, and redefine our targets.

Using this simple methodology we look at what transformations we are trying to make. If we make quite simple predictions about what we are trying to do, and how we're doing it, then we can see if it's worked. This point is emphasized again here because, although evaluation is often tagged on to the end of any process, formative evaluation needs to be considered right at the beginning. Our evaluation tightens up our change efforts. It helps us to be more exact about what kind of transformations we will be making, and then to measure how effecctive they have been. The answers to these structured questions constitute the information we need to reappraise the effect, and see whether to adjust the process.

Exercise 1: Evaluation

The process of evaluation is much easier if you consider a real example. Readers should start by working on an example unrelated to their own practice. For example: What is a garage for?

1. Describe its functions (for example, to mend my car, to tow in broken down vehicles, to sell cars).

---

2. What operations does it undertake to do the above (for example, mechanics work on the cars, they take my money)?

---

3. Would the way you described these two be useful to measure an improvement in the garage's performance? (Unless you can get a tight definition of the operations it undertakes, and the purposes of those operations, then the definition will not be useful in improving their performance. That's why evaluation is useful – to see how we're doing. Using such an example in a structured way should be useful in developing your own evaluation skills.)

Exercise 2: Evaluation

Now try the example of the garage using the transformation process.
You are going to structure the purposeful activities of the garage so
they relate inputs to outputs.

Purposeful
In ────────────────► activity ──────────────────► Out
(transformation)

1. What is the garage there for?

    (a) To take faulty cars *in* and to send functioning cars *out*
    (b) To take *in* new spare parts in their packets and to send the
    parts *out* in cars

In   *Are transformed:*   *Out*

New parts in packets ────────► Into ──────────► New parts in cars

Faulty cars ──────────────► Into ──────────► Functioning cars

───

───

2. Now you will need to specify what happens (the purposeful
   activity) and how this transforms the input to output. In our
   example, what is it that transforms new parts in packets to new
   parts in cars? Try to do it yourself.

Input: New parts in packets   *Output:* New parts in cars

─────────────────────────   ─────────────────────────

─────────────────────────   ─────────────────────────

Practise this process by noting down other inputs (for example,
money in my pocket) and their related outputs (for example, money
in the garage till). Next specify the activity or transformation that
makes this change.

Input   *Purposeful activity*   *Output*
                 (transformation)

──────────   ─────────────────────────   ──────────────

──────────   ─────────────────────────   ──────────────

Remember that, for the sake of the technique, the output can only be
the transformed input. For example, if your input is a burst tyre, your
output can't be a new windscreen! A burst tyre can become a
functioning tyre; a broken windscreen can become a new
windscreen. Once you have specified the transformation, then you
are beginning to learn to define performance and the changes you
want. Specifying that performance in small and operationally defined
bits will help to see if the organization is doing its job.

The most common problem with evaluation is that transformations are defined too generally. If you said earlier that the garage's function was to mend cars, it will be difficult to measure this, because it is too general. Two observers would probably not agree on what this meant, and therefore we would be unsure whether the garage was doing its job or not. Try the exercise again bearing this in mind.

Input	*Output*
Dirty cars	Clean cars
New parts in packets	New parts in cars
Money in customers' pockets	Money in garage till
Dented body work	Smooth body work

Now specify how the transformation takes place (for example, how does it turn dirty cars into clean cars?). For instance, a trainee washes four cars by hand, every day, using eight buckets of water and three types of chemicals.

Now you need to check these transformations against three criteria:

- *efficacy:* did our method do what was intended? (Did the dirty car end up clean, to a certain standard?)
- *efficiency:* what resources were used? Could we have done it with less people, cheaper, quicker? (Is employing a trainee the most efficient method of doing the job, or would a more experienced person have done five or six a day? Chat up the customers less? Use less chemicals?)
- *effectiveness:* is it worth cleaning cars? (Is this the sort of thing we want to be doing in this garage? Does it fit our core mission?)

For the last criterion (effectiveness), you will need to search beyond the immediate environment and to related systems. For instance, when we question our effectiveness we need to ask questions like: do clean cars give a good public image to our garage? Do they cause less accidents on the road? Do they reduce rust? Effectiveness involves boundary systems, like the police, the public, and so on.

Exercise 3: Evaluation

Now you can try an exercise related to your own work area.

1. What is your department/ward/unit here for? (If you make the mission very general – for example, to cure people – you will find it difficult to specify the transformation/activities that you are trying to make to transform the input to output. So define it tightly and operationally.)

2. What are the inputs and outputs?

_____

_____

3. What are the transformations/activities you undertake to do this?

_____

_____

4. Are these:
   (a) Efficacious? Do they do the intended job?
   (b) Efficient? Do they do it the cheapest, fastest way?
   (c) Effective? Is it worth doing?

Now try the following full change exercise, with your own issues and/or problems.

Exercise 4: Creating change from within: systematic diagnosis of the problem and the system

1. What business is your department/unit in and what is your role in this? Specify your mission.

_____

_____

2. What is the future vision?

_____

_____

3. What are the key domains? What are the demands they are making and the responses your unit is making? (Imagine it's a person you're taking to – What are they asking for? How do you reply?)

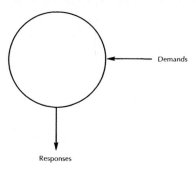

Demands

Responses

Demands: _____

_____

Responses: _____

_____

4. What types of change are needed? Attitudes, behaviour, policies, practices?

_____

_____

5. What parts of the system and which key people are relevant to this particular change? (Try the planned technique.)
Example:

```
                    ┌──────────┐
                    │ Dr   X   │
                    │ Trainer  │
                    └──────────┘
                         ╲
                    ╭──────────╮
                    │Fundholding│
                    │ GPs   XX │
                    ╰──────────╯          ┌──────────────────┐
                         │               │ Health Commission│
                         │               │ Purchaser  X     │
   ┌────────┐            ▼               └──────────────────┘
   │ CHC    │       ╭──────────╮
   │ Sec  X │──────▶│Psychology│◀─────    ┌──────────────┐
   └────────┘       │department│          │ Social       │
                    ╰──────────╯          │ Services     │
                         ▲                ├──────────────┤
   ┌──────────┐          │               │ Mental Health │
   │ Mind  X  │          │               │ & Business    │
   ├──────────┤          │               │ Managers  XX  │
   │ MENCAP X │          │               └──────────────┘
   └──────────┘          │
                         │               ┌──────────────┐
                    ┌──────────┐         │Psychiatrists XX│
                    │ Employee │         └──────────────┘
                    │Assistance│
                    │ Ltd      │
                    └──────────┘
```

Key
← Factors affecting the department
X = Key people
    (What is their condition?
        their energy?
        their commitment?
        their competence?)

6. Which areas 'fit' best and worst?

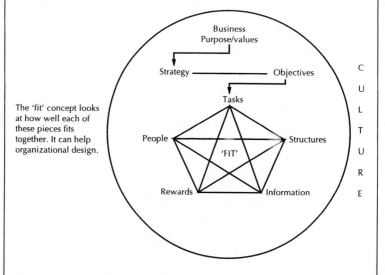

The 'fit' concept looks at how well each of these pieces fits together. It can help organizational design.

- Which need improving?

7. What are the forces for and against this change? This can be called forcefield analysis, where you list all the domains (including people) and see whether they are for or against your change. Some may straddle the two sides.

Forces for the change →   *Change*   ← *Forces against the change*

_____   _____

_____   _____

Which are more/less important? Underline the most important one to address.
Removing forces against should be tried first.

8. Is this change realistic? Do you need to change your goal?

_____

_____

9. What are the reasons for wanting change?
Personal: _____

_____

Organizational: _____

_____

10. What influence can you have in this change process?

Formal: _____

_____

Informal: _____

_____

11. How can you exert leverage? Consider the change equation here:

$$\text{Different future vision} \times \text{Dissatisfaction with current state} \times \text{First steps} > \text{Cost of change}$$

Where are the weaknesses? (You need all three to overcome the cost of change.)

_____

_____

12. Is there a domino effect? (Maybe you can create a sequence of change, by choosing your first move carefully.)

_____

_____

Exercise 5: Creating change from within: building up a clearer vision of the future

This exercise involves working on your key domains.

1. Check what demands you expect will be made on your department in the future and what responses you would like.

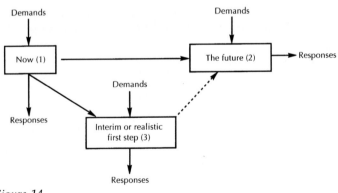

Figure 14

(Try to visualize the helicopter view of your future. What does it look like down there? What's changed? Try different futures. Remember that multiple scenarios are your best way of planning for the unexpected, in these changing times.) See whether the demands and responses are very far apart. If the distance between the demands and the responses is too far, then make stepwise reductions until your first step seems achievable (see Figure 14). Now you have a realistic change target (in your realistic first step).

2. So what changes are needed?

   (a) *Environmental mapping*: you will need to do this again because you have now specified what your first change step is. Start mapping the demands and responses, and the key people and key domains, simply in relation to your first step.
   (b) *Identify organization areas*: plot the key people and the key domains for this change target.

   You have now identified the key people and the systems involved in your new change goals. Now you need to decide what is their state of readiness and capability. Fill in the following table as it applies to your situation, ranking (High, Medium, Low) each individual or group necessary for your change effort according to their readiness and their capability with respect in the change:

Key people/system	*Readiness*			*Capability*		
	H	M	L	H	M	L
_____	___	___	___	___	___	___
_____	___	___	___	___	___	___

This exercise will focus your efforts in creating energy in others, for change. You are now identifying a critical mass and people with commitment to the change.

   Forcefield analysis will now help you clarify the systems involved, your allies and blocks. You might try this now in relation to your future scenario, as you did before in relation to the general changes.

What and who is driving the change?   *What and who is hindering the change?*

————————————————→ ←————————————————
————————————————→ ←————————————————

- Check this against your domains – people, systems, media, legislation.

3. What do you bring to the change effort?

   (a) What is your power and your ability to influence in this organization?

   _____

   _____

(b) How can you influence others? (Who might have more power than you? What are the incentives or pressures?)

_____

_____

(c) Why do you want these particular changes? Is it to improve effectiveness? To increase regional interest in centralizing specialist services in your hospital? To increase efficiency? To reduce complaints? Or are your reasons more personal? To improve your career prospects? To create a more interesting work environment for you? You will need to defend your moves to other people, so be quite clear on your own motives. If they are too heavily weighted towards the personal, then you may be seen as too selfish or 'empire building', and not an organization person!

If you remind yourself of the section on 'readiness to change', you will see that key people will need to be in a state of personal and organizational health, to be able to take on the changes. It is costly for people to change, so you will need to support them and make it rewarding if they are to drive or support your changes.

(d) List your own personal motives for wanting these changes.

_____

_____

● If you are trying to influence other people, it will be a lot easier if you are clear about your own motives for change. You can then discuss your reasons with them and draw out their reasons for wanting change.

It is important to remind the reader here that transition is often characterized by high uncertainty, high emotional stress, high energy and increased conflict. It is the healthiness of the organization and of the individuals in it that determines a good outcome, because change demands a high tolerance of uncertainty. The reader can use the 'health of the organization questionnaire' in Appendix B to give a good indication of the level of security, which can help you to determine the likelihood of success. It can also give you some ideas on the work necessary to get the organization into a reasonable state of healthiness and receptivity before starting the change effort.

It may also be useful to look at the 'role effectiveness questionnaire' (in Appendix C). This questionnaire is useful in giving you, as a manager, some ideas of the problems key people are having with their current role and their satisfaction with it. Dissatisfied people can energize a system, but very high levels of either satisfaction or dissatisfaction can reduce people's contribution to the change effort. They become impotent and ineffectual.

You might like to read Appendix D on Support and Challenge, a way to understand how to manage different levels of security in different people – to lead to high performance.

Plans need to be developed to cover changes in tasks, formal and informal systems, and individuals. A consistent approach is needed for all of these four major areas. The section on transition planning (see Chapter 1) outlines the usual stages in some detail. For your own purposes here, these stages have been designed as a personal exercise

---

Exercise 6: Creating change from within: action plan for building commitment and initiating change

1. Try to list the changes that you anticipate in these four major areas over the transition period.

   Tasks: _____

   _____

   Formal systems: _____

   _____

   Informal systems: _____

   _____

   Individuals: _____

   _____

2. Indicate how you are going to prepare individuals and boundary systems for the uncertainty and difficulties you anticipate. Strong leadership and a shared expectation of unsettlement and uncertainty will help.

   Preparing individual: _____

   _____

   Preparing boundaries: _____

   _____

3. Communication systems need to be able to cope with these major changes by making roles and responsibilities clear during the change process and by giving performance feedback so that even small successes can be rewarded. What are your plans for:

   (a) Clarifying roles/responsibilities?

   _____

   _____

   (b) Giving feedback?

   _____

   _____

4. What kind of formal plans are you making for the transition? Do you wish to appoint a project manager, to enlarge the role of one of your senior members, or to release yourself from some of your current duties so you can have more time for the change process? What new structure have you planned?

   _____

   _____

5. Identify individuals whose commitment is needed for your change. Then check what their current state of commitment is. Can you shift them to a more supportive position?

   Key person   *Commitment (current: x; potential;√)*

                        Oppose Let   Support   Make it happen

   _____ _____ _____ _____

   _____ _____ _____ _____

   • Develop a plan for getting the necessary commitment from the critical mass. You may need to find an activity that loosens up the group, unfreezing current attitudes. For example, a problem-finding task – a kind of 'think tank; where brainstorming is encouraged/allowed and any problem is discussed – in confidence!) What are *your* plans for getting the group to work together on this new project?

   _____

6. How are you developing rewards so new behaviours can be encouraged? Perhaps you can function as a role model – so others can see you reward your staff for doing things differently or trying our new ideas.

   _____

   _____

7. It may be useful for your group to use a task analysis table in planning the tasks. Actors are listed across the top and tasks down the left-hand column. The table is completed by noting the

particular role for each key player: approval support, informed, responsible, for example. This is a useful tool for identifying exactly who is responsible for what action during the transition period. If possible, keep those *responsible* to a minimum (one preferably). (Relate this back to your commitment charting; it is not useful to have somebody responsible for a key task who is not highly committed.)

It is useful to develop this table together with the group, sharing the idea and minimizing the numbers responsible. This also tests out, with your group ('your critical mass'), whether you really have a common understanding and appreciation of each other's roles, and where responsibility lies.

8. Check that your action plan is:
   (a) Purposeful: are you going to end up at the right place?
   (b) Specific: not so general, it will cause confusion.
   (c) Integrated: different parts of the plan relate together well.
   (d) Timed: you have fixed dates for actions.
   (e) Adaptable: allows for changes.
   (f) Cost effective: the cheapest way to do the job.

● State your action plans:

Task   *Names*

_____   _____

_____   _____

Although a systematic plan is recommended, it should be subject to constant review by your group. It is likely to need changing as you go along.

9. How will you know whether your intervention has worked? List your inputs and outputs for the future.

Input   *Output*

_____   _____

_____   _____

Then add your purposeful activities to get there.

In   *Purposeful activity*   *Out*

_____   _____   _____

_____   _____   _____

● Check that your plan is likely to achieve the desired outcome and that it is going to get the job done (*efficacious*); is the best way of doing it (*efficient*); and is worth doing (*effective*). NOW TRY DOING IT!

References

1. Marson, S., (eds.), *Managing People* (Macmillan, 1990).
2. Belbin, R. M., *Management Teams – Why They Succeed or Fail* (Heinemann, 1981).
3. Mintzberg, H., *The Nature of Managerial Work* (Prentice-Hall, 1973).
4. Walton, M., *Management and Managing: A Dynamic Approach* (Harper & Row, 1984).
5. Burns, J. M., *Leadership* (Harper & Row, 1978).
6. Turrell, E. A., *Change and Innovation: a Challenge for the NHS* (IHSM, 1986).
7. Benis, G. W., *et al.*, *The Planning of Change* (Holt, Rinehart & Winston, 1976).
8. Adair, J., *Effective Team-Building* (Pan, 1986).
9. Lancaster, J., and W. Lancaster, *The Nurse as a Change Agent* (Mosby, 1982).
10. Plant, R., *Making Change and Making it Stick* (Fontana, 1987).
11. Tichy, N. M., and M. A. Devanna, 'The Transformational Leader', *Training and Development Journal* (July 1986).
12. Gawlinski, G., and L. Graessle, *Planning Together. The Art of Effective Teamwork* (Bedford Square Press, 1988).
13. Critchley, B., and D. Casey, 'Second Thoughts on Team Building', *Management Education and Development* (1984) **15**(2), 163–75.
14. Checkland, P., *Systems Thinking, Systems Practice* (Wiley, 1981).
15. Ibid.
16. Ibid.

Chapter 3   Imposed Change

This chapter concentrates on the opportunities for change that can be created by external pressures and demands. Although these sorts of changes are often resisted, they can act as a catalyst and be used to the organization's advantage. However, the ability to respond to such a catalyst will depend on the people in it, their state of confidence and their readiness for change. The principles of using imposed changes will be demonstrated through a case study.

Case study 8

The work of pathology departments has undergone significant changes over recent years, with dramatic developments in technology and mechanization of processes that previously needed skilled 'hands-on' operators. In our example department, there had been a significant competitive market developing and a fall-off in recruitment in the scientific officer grades, since the NHS salaries were not as attractive in comparison to the private sector salaries available locally. The department was having to rethink its internal organization, grading structure and working methods to take account of the changing skills needed. In addition, the purchasers had increased the pressure on the department by offering much tighter contracts, until costs all reduced. The Business manager asked the Head Pathologist:

- to review the current operation of the department
- to draft workable options for the future structure in the department, while improving standards and maintaining activity levels, and reducing unit costs.

The Business manager thought that the pathology department probably had excess capacity, in plant and equipment, but he was unsure of the strength of human resources. He put pressure on the head of department to make changes.

> The head of department was already feeling particularly pressurized by staff shortages, and the imposed changes were a bolt out of the blue. She felt quite unsure how to tackle the issues and had even considered leaving the service herself when faced with what she felt was overwhelming pressure.

Diagnosis of Readiness to Change

When this process of imposed change is compared to change from within, it is clear that a major issue is about *ownership*. When those closely involved do not 'own' the pressures or the changes, it is likely they will react with shock and helplessness.

Figure 15 shows the delicate balance needed to bring key individuals into a state of readiness. There will be individual features (self-esteem, ability to adapt, dissatisfaction, and so on) that make them more or less ready to take on new ideas, but there will also be organizational forces. Some companies or hospitals are used to change, so there is a togetherness in the way each new pressure is received. They respond with 'What can we do to make it work?' rather than 'How can we resist it?' Together, these two factors (individual state and culture) will combine to give a measure of readiness. If this is very low or very high, then change is unlikely.

We can also expect that, if resistance is increased, the old system will be 'over-valued'. On occasions, unpredictable and novel behaviours will also be seen.

But unplanned or imposed change, by its nature, does not start by people building a common vision of the future. The key players need to come 'on board' and start to work together towards the same goals as quickly as possible, and begin to drive the process, so they find some positives in it.

Returning to our pathology example, the head of department felt particularly pressurized and threatened. She was overwhelmed by the changes suggested and saw it as threatening her control and power. She resisted the change – 'I wasn't employed to do this.' It was quite clear that she did not feel part of the change process, and that she felt she was losing influence and control in planning the department's future. The

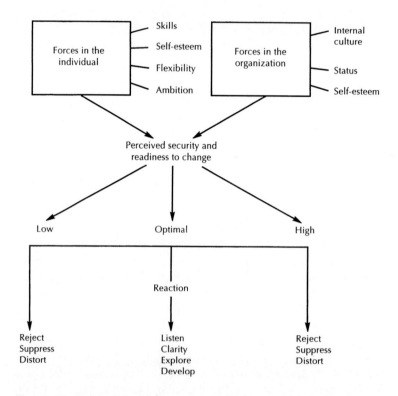

Figure 15 Estimating readiness to respond to imposed change

pressure had become intense for this one individual. Her reaction was classic and over the next few weeks she demonstrated the usual stages of shock – beginning with anger and elation:

Shock→Elation→Denial→Withdrawal→Acknowledgement→Adaptation

The Pain of Change for the Individual

Remember the phrase 'No pain, no gain'? Changes are rarely achieved without some pain, but it is up to the manager to utilize their skills so that the pain and energy generated in

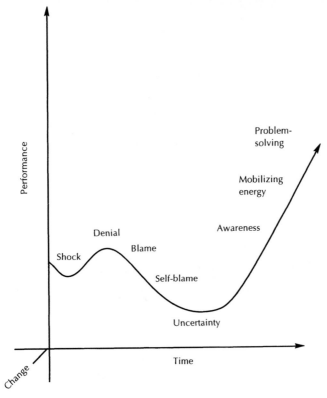

Figure 16 Imposed/unplanned change: effects on people

individuals in the organization by outside pressures is used to drive the changes.

In psychological jargon, such imposed pressures can create *dissonance* (see Chapter 1). This can be defined as the uncertainty or unsettlement that comes from a mismatch between the way things *are* and the way they *could* be, or you want them to be. Dissonance is an active word; it describes the energy necessary to reduce the mismatch. There seems to be a human need to reduce dissonance; that is, to return to a more stable state – an equilibrium. The 'energy' can be directed into creating new structures, new attitudes and new processes. However, a less constructive way of reducing dissonance is to

REACTION	EXPRESSION
Shock	Numbness 'I can't take it in.' Feeling of unreality Distance
Denial	'It's not that different.' 'I don't believe you.' 'This is really simple.' 'I must have heard wrong.' 'That can't be right.'
Blame	'It's everyone else's fault.' 'They don't know what they're doing.' 'If only they had listened to me.' 'They never handle anything well here.' 'You never liked me.'
Self-blame	'I'm too old.' 'If only I'd taken it more seriously.' 'I can't adapt.' 'It's all my fault.'
Uncertainty	'What's happening to me?' 'Why am I doing this?' 'I'm not sure what to do.'
Problem-solving	'What shall I do about it?' 'Let's take stock here.' 'What I think would help is . . .' 'Perhaps I could talk to my old boss.'

Figure 17 Human response to change

return to the old ways of doing things. Managers may, at times, be tempted not to use these changes and let things return to 'normal', simply because the pain is too great and the cost of change too high.

● *How can managers help to reduce the costs, but use the disso-nance to create change?* First, they can help people anticipate the upset and accommodate to it. They can acknowledge the reaction, while encouraging people to stay with it and not allow them 'off the hook'. There is a parallel here to the shock of

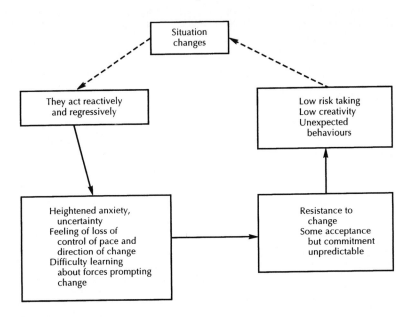

Figure 18 Human response to change

bereavement and loss, when individuals will go through a variety of stages – like shock, anger, resentment, guilt, depression, and so on. However, this reaction will, as in our current example, depend on their own healthiness and skills at coping.

Second, some continuity can help each individual to manage the changes. For instance, the head of service had always kept a high profile as a union representative on the senior staff committee. This role was maintained by the Business manager, to reassure the head of department that not all arenas had been changing at the same time, and that change was only expected in one area. (Remember the four arenas – tasks, formal and informal structures, and individuals?)

Our head pathologist had some sophistication in change processes and she began to acknowledge that, although the pressure she was under was highly painful, it could be turned to advantage. The Business manager listened to her anger and resentment, and the two together began to review their current relationship, the pressures on them and the possibilities for change. They had taken the first step in a major change process and the head pathologist was beginning to use her efforts to drive the changes in a direction she wanted. She was beginning to *own* the process.

1. Stress at work

Although other volumes in this series are concerned with the details of stress and self-management,[1] it is rightly included here because the changes described, whether imposed by external factors or created from within, will all create personal dissonance and *stress*. The amount of *strain* that people feel will depend on their own psychological state, but work systems can also create stress which may pressurize individuals. If the level of work stress is high, this can affect the potential for change that can be expected.

It may be useful here simply to list work-related pressures that lead to high stress, as gleaned from the literature. You can then use it as a checklist.

- *Time*: non-standard working hours; deadlines to meet and unreasonable time demands
- *Work setting*: heavy workload and overload; responsibility load; red tape; monotony; over-participation/over-involvement; poor labour relations
- *Role-related*: role conflict (see 'Role Effectiveness Inventory' in Appendix C); degree or control over work processes; feedback and communication problems; poor relationships with superiors; inequality or inadequacy of pay; quantity/quality conflict
- *Changes in job*: job complexity; loss of job or fear or loss; demotion; over-promotion; lack of promotion opportunities.

This list will be useful in estimating people's readiness to change, and also when managers want to design a healthy work environment that has a greater potential for change.

2. Using the pain to make gains

Let's return to our head pathologist, who is feeling shocked, but who knows that changes will have to be made, since the outside pressures are clearly not going to go away. She has certain choices, and so she begins to work with the key people in the department, to see whether her department is ready for change. She estimates that the pressures are high, but her colleagues are robust; they have shown a certain strength under pressure before. She begins to work with them on building up commitment for change, and then works with key staff from other related departments to begin to define options for more efficient work practices, and so to be more competitive on cost and quality.

It might pay to remind readers at this moment of the basic change questions which the head of department could ask, when attempting to use this unsettled or 'dissonant' stage to begin a successful change process.

- What is the current state?
- What are the problems with the current state?
- What will happen if we don't change anything? (Use planned neglect technique.)
- Change from what (now); to what (the future)?
- What systems are we trying to change?
- Who are the key people? What is their commitment and energy?
- What are the key boundaries to be managed?
- What structures and roles are needed to manage the changes? (Transition plans)
- How will we know how well we're doing? (Evaluation)

The processes and tools in Figure 19 are described as they apply to each stage. For instance, the technique of forcefield analysis is most useful when the desired future state is beginning to be worked up – at that time, it is essential to estimate the important forces 'for' and 'against'.

Our head pathologist is now faced with a system that is (levered) ready for change. There is already some pain and energy created by the pressures from outside, and the change process now becomes similar to that outlined in Chapter 2 – once she owns the process herself and begins to build commitment around her, then the processes are similar to internal change processes.

It may be useful at this point to note the most common causes of failure of organizational change.[2]

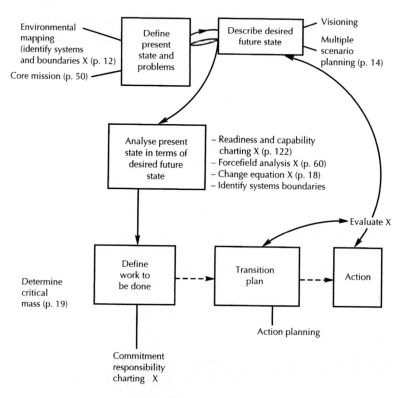

Figure 19 The process of change

- incomplete diagnosis
- starting off too fast (and losing the strategic connection)
- missionary zeal; the 'flavour of the month'
- losing the senior sponsor
- lack of steering from the steering group
- moving too fast for people to absorb the consequences
- placing demands for (unrealistic) short-term results
- failing to evaluate benefits as they occur
- not monitoring the boundaries
- failing to get key players in the right state of commitment and support

- insufficient involvement of the people affected by the changes
- insufficient resources allocated to maintain the programme.

This highlights the need to get the 'key players in the right condition' so they lead the changes. Without the head of department's 'ownership' the pathology department is unlikely to make changes and survive.

Unplanned Change

When there is a general culture of innovation and change, the unexpected catalyst can be productive, and the organization can take advantage of the dissonance it creates. This can only happen if the key players are in a state of energy and influence, so they will act proactively and feel comfortable with the stages of change, rather than overwhelmed by the unknown. In a dynamic culture, they will be more used to risk taking (see Figure 20).

However, if the organization is unused to change and has a low tolerance for change, then individuals will suffer more during imposed change. They may feel loss of control and will make efforts to restore their own equilibrium and control of the situation. They may show low risk taking and a preference for the traditional ways of doing things (see Figure 21). For instance, while working in one mental health Trust, the Chief Executive could not get general commitment to her formal plans to close a mental hospital. Taking a pragmatic, 'top-down' style, she began to impose the first changes without the commitment of the 'key' health service staff affected and the boundary agencies involved (like the local GP's, who wanted extra payments to cover the patients' medical needs once they were in the community). Because these changes were imposed rather than developed with key people, and the appropriate stages of commitment building had not been worked on, there were all kinds of resistance. The GPs resorted to the local press, the BMA and the MDU for discussions about rules for extra responsibility payment. Social services published alternative 'plans for action'.

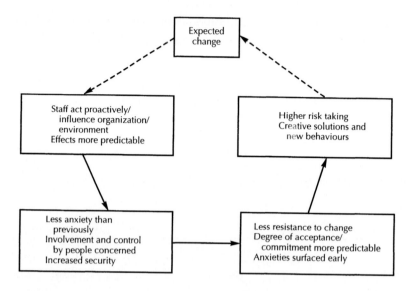

Figure 20 Planned change: effects on people

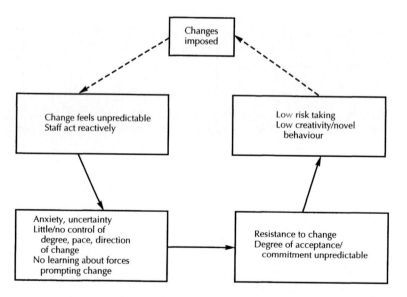

Figure 21 Unplanned change: effects on people

Figure 22 builds on the change equation to show how to focus on the three areas of leverage, to increase readiness to change. In the mental health case, we can see that a new future vision was needed and that key people needed to *own* it. Resistance will be less likely if the forces in the individual and the system are prepared and committed to change. However, the costs of change are usually high, and each of the three areas need to be worked on:

- a different vision of the future
- dissatisfaction with the present
- achievable first steps.

It may be useful here to remind the reader of the value of creating a *general* culture of change. This would make the system readier to take up new ideas, whether planned or unplanned, or coming from external sources. Please see Figures 16 (p. 71) and 17 (p. 72), which describe, very generally, the process of response to change which people go through variably as change occurs. It is possible to see these changes both in yourself and in other people. It is a normal reaction to go through, sometimes in quite an extended way. The parallels with the bereavement process will be noticeable to the perceptive reader.

Assessing Readiness to Change

Figure 23 attempts to bring together in diagrammatic form some of the individual and system forces you need to identify when assessing readiness to change.

1. The individual

Readers will note that some of the forces in the individual can be developed through traditional training methods (motivation/skills and knowledge), but some seem to exist as more personal characteristics (tolerance of ambiguity/self-esteem). This highlights the need for the manager to take responsibility for helping staff to *develop*, rather than just *training* them in skills.

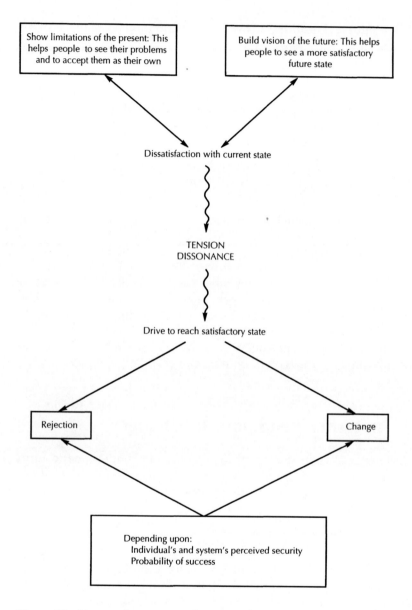

Figure 22 How to increase readiness to change

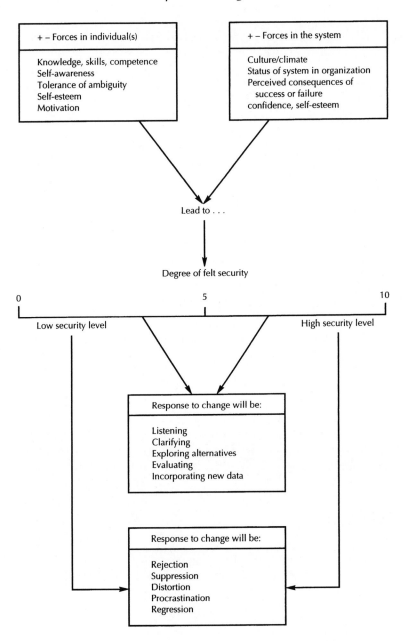

Figure 23 Diagnosing readiness to change

2. The system

Even if the system has developed a culture of change, as discussed earlier, there are still other factors to consider in estimating the likelihood of change. For instance, one learning disabilities unit had such high regard locally that a brave plan was estimated to have a high chance of success as a change. The service was perceived locally as an efficient, confident and caring service; one that was continually reviewing and experimenting. In this context, one failure for a generally innovative system would not be such a disaster; it would have been seen as a good learning experience. However, it was not an option the board had discussed.

Of course, these two aspects, the individual and the system, will interact, depending on the appropriate level of challenge and support (see Appendix D). For instance, the individual's tolerance for ambiguity can increase if there is strong support from colleagues. Similarly, if the system supports experiment and risk, people who normally have a low tolerance for ambiguity will tend to work at a higher level of uncertainty. For example, in our pathology example, increasing the research and development (R&D) component for the service's scientific officers would increase the problem-finding and problem-solving component of their job, their job satisfaction and reduce their repetitive work. Their interest in the job would therefore increase and so turnover would reduce and services would improve. This R&D could also produce marketable products, which could soon improve the financial rewards for staff in bonus payments.

References

1. Tschudin, U., *Managing Yourself* (Macmillan, 1990).
2. Moscow, D., 'Effective Implementation of Organization Development in the NHS', *Health Service Manpower Review* (1986) **12** (2), 3–7.

Chapter 4   The Nurse as a Change Agent

If we compare two rather different strategies that a change agent might use – *coercion* and *participation* – the attentive reader will notice that the latter is my preferred option, since it empowers participants and they own the changes. However, where the power is clear and the change agent has control of the rewards, then coercion can be effective, although it is prescriptive and tends to reduce the contribution that staff can make to the change process. Indeed, sometimes, due to very short time demands, it is essential. This chapter considers the various roles of the change agent and, through an in-depth case study, demonstrates the way the participative style can be used, by an external change agent.

The Nurse in the System

In the current complexity of the NHS, the nursing profession provides a backbone of continuity to service delivery. Nurses have an in-depth knowledge and familiarity of the system, and have a role of influence and responsibility that is fairly formally defined and well understood, although it has been argued that nursing as a profession does not always fully exploit this power! So it could be argued that the position of nurses in the system is more suited to the coercive approach than the participative. The demonstrate the difference, we will observe two different approaches to the same problem.

Case study 9

A ward manager is told that surgical patients need more information and preparation for their operations. There have been a stream of complaints, misunderstandings and heated discussion between patients, their relatives and staff.

Using a *coercive* approach, the ward manager might instruct all contact staff to spend twenty minutes preparing each patients 'and I will check that you have done it'.

If, on the other hand, the ward manager adopts a participative approach, she might focus discussion on the issue with her staff, raise concern about current performance (in terms of the change equation, she might start by *increasing dissatisfaction with the present*) and work with the team to develop a common vision and commitment to change. After developing this commitment, the staff would be encouraged to define the changes and to find the most effective way of achieving the agreed changes. They might all become involved in measuring and sharing feedback on how they were doing.

It is evident from this example that the coercive approach can be immediately effective (when the ward manager is watching!), but the participate approach is generally favoured here, since it helps the staff learn together, and the changes are owned by those implementing them. The conclusion therefore might be that it is more natural to step into a coercive approach in a hierarchical system, or if time is short. But, if we are concerned with developing a renewing organization, an organization that has a general change climate, then the participative approach might be seen as a better investment. Of course, the major staff resource of the health service is the nurses, so their ability to take on change issues is important for the future of the NHS.

Stress, Strain and Coping

It is the balance of individuals' internal state and skill, and the support and encouragement they receive from their surroundings, that will determine their capacity to deal with uncertainty. If individuals are put under too much pressure,

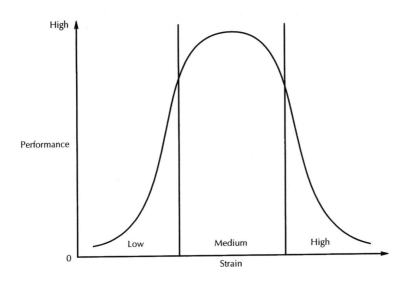

Figure 24 Performance at different levels of stress

they will resist change, but if they are part of an organization that values change, then they are more likely to take risks and to contribute more to the change effort.

But the behaviour of individuals is a product of the pressors they feel (*stress*) and their own adaptive ability (*coping*). People can affect the level of strain they feel by manipulating either the pressors (by changing work practice) or their adaptation (by training). If there are excessive pressors in work and home life, and individuals have few coping skills, then they will feel *strain*. If they are strained, they have less capacity to contribute energy to the demands of the change process. On the other hand, individuals who are highly adaptable and welcome challenge may welcome new challenges. To the outsider, they may appear to have more than their fair share of stressors, but this is a very individual matter.

Figure 24 shows the usual effects of stress on performance. With higher stress, the lower the performance. However, a very low level of arousal (or stress) also produces a poor performance.

So is it important to build a general culture of change in your organization? It is in such an environment that adapting

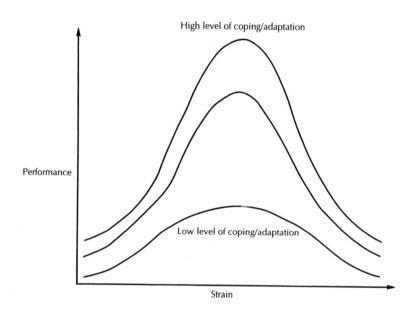

Figure 25 Different levels of performance varying with adaptation skills

to the new becomes a part of life and the process of change is the norm. In a renewing culture, the skill of adaptation becomes well developed and people can withstand high levels of pressors.

In order to maintain a workable level of stress for themselves, individuals will either resist or welcome changes. If they resist, it might be because they feel close to their threshold for stress. When under pressure, people do not have the capacity to cope with anything more (see Figure 25). For example, working women, who comprise a high proportion of nursing staff, often have a set of culturally determined pressors. Many have to do their housework and care for their family while maintaining a full-time job. If one of their children is ill, they have to arrange for a substitute carer before rushing off to work, decide if a doctor is needed and then they are preoccupied about the child's health while at work. They therefore have a high level of pressors on them. Some men too may face these pressors. However, much more commonly, men would not have the nurturing responsibilities and the preoccupation this might cause at work, which gives women stress. It is quite clear that a woman's capacity to deal with new and challenging situations on a day like this would be rather reduced.

This example highlights the need to consider the total environment of each individual when looking at a person's capacity to join in the change process and to perform at the highest level. When we say 'the total environment' we should include not only the complex of the work organization, but also the private and personal responsibilities and stressors that people bring with them. All this will affect their capacity to take on new ideas, new behaviours and new practices. On one day, a person's capacity might be much greater than on another, due to the wide range of straining factors. A good manager will be in touch with these factors, note the individual's capacity to take on new challenges at different times and will match the change process accordingly.

In analysing an individual's capacity, there is no room for blame. It is preferable to understand the complex processes and learn to deal with them. The good manager and change agent will be able to estimate and discuss an individual's capacity for change, and the likelihood of success. For the manager, this will come from their knowledge and concern for the individuals that work with them, and the openness of their relationship. It is clear that many change efforts fail because of a mismatch of the demands it places on individuals and their capacity, at that time, to deal with them.

What is a Change Agent?

The formal definition of a change agent might be: 'Someone who identifies major problem areas, identifies the opportunities for change, builds readiness and commitment, builds a renewing system through creating a climate for change, and establishes internal capacity to sustain the change effort, evaluate and review it.' However, individual change agents will clearly have different skills and preferences. The continuum of managerial behaviour (see Figure 26) shows the wide range of expert skills that a manager, as change agent, might use. The skill is in matching these with the needs of each situation.

For instance, it may be more appropriate if the change agent is building a climate of review and innovation for them to take a *facilitating* role. However, if the organization wants an expert system established (for example, an information system to monitor the costs of an operating theatre), it might be more appropriate for the change agent to adopt the *expert* role, and get the system 'up and running', because otherwise the knottier crisis issue of overspending might interfere with the long-term project aim of building up commitment for a more efficient service. Clearly, the different roles must be openly negotiated. It is important to be aware of this continuum and of the choices you might have when you make and undertake negotiations. You can only move up and down the continuum if you have the skills ready and waiting!

There are different ways of promoting change, and there are also different types of change agent. The three prevalent models will be described here.

1. External change agent
2. Internal change agent
3. Employee as change agent

1. External change agent

The Health Service is getting more used to employing external organization development (OD) consultants. Such outsiders have the advantage that they are external to the system, and often they will operate at the facilitating (process) end of the continuum, helping to clarify the position and problems, and work on options. External process consultants, like myself, might work on the types of projects described throughout this book, but also perhaps on building internal processes, like team-building or facilitating strategic planning, where outsiders are valued for their process skills in helping the organization develop its own capacity for change.

External expert consultants are also increasingly employed,

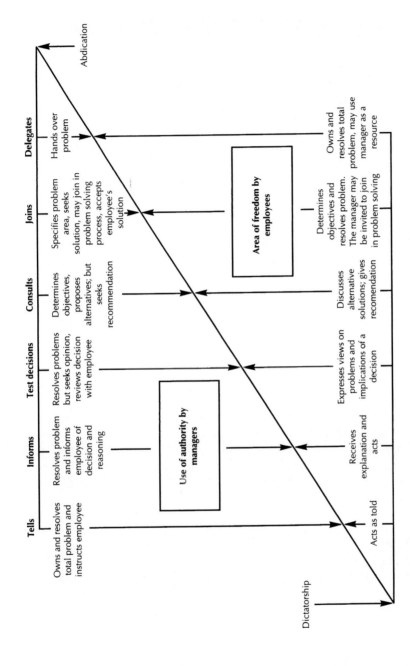

Tells | Informs | Test decisions | Consults | Joins | Delegates

Tells
Owns and resolves total problem and instructs employee

Informs
Resolves problem and informs employee of decision and reasoning

Test decisions
Resolves problems but seeks opinion, reviews decision with employee

Consults
Determines objectives, proposes alternatives; but seeks recommendation

Joins
Specifies problem area, seeks solution, may join in problem solving process, accepts employee's solution

Delegates
Hands over problem

Abdication

Area of freedom by employees

Use of authority by managers

Acts as told

Receives explanation and acts

Expresses views on problems and implications of a decision

Discusses alternative solutions; gives recomendation

Determines objectives and resolves problem. The manager may be invited to join in problem solving

Owns and resolves total problem, may use manager as a resource

Dictatorship

Figure 26 Continuum of managerial behaviour

89

although they are not so pertinent to this book, since their input is less concerned with facilitating the organization's strengths in managing change than in prescribing solutions. They will tend to be employed on technical projects, such as installing information systems or estimating manpower needed for a new general hospital.

Some readers may have been employed in the external change agent role or may be considering moving into this area of work. They will realize that there are added advantages to being outside the system. These include the wide perspective this gives and the opportunity to act as 'honest broker' on behalf of the client, with other agencies and key people.

On the negative side, there is, on occasions, a disadvantage when the client or key people have to explain to an outside consultant, in some detail, things that they and their colleagues understand as if by osmosis, simply by being part of the system. This is less of a problem with process consultation than with expert consultancy. In the latter, detailed knowledge of the service is essential.

2. Internal change agent

Internal change agents have the advantage of knowing about the personnel, the current culture, the language and the local issues. However, they do not have the detachment, and on occasions they don't have the wide perspective of the external consultant, the benchmark and message-carrying role. Discussing their role with some of the NHS internal change advisers, it does appear that some of them find it difficult to adopt different positions in the organization on different change projects. For example, they may be a *catalyst* in one project, the *confidante* of the client in another and a *coach* in another. It is difficult for both the change agent and others in the organization relating to them to have to shift their behaviour and roles for the same people in different projects.

The author is familiar with internal change agents who have used their role well, by adopting some of the catalytic role while maintaining their internal professional status, and have initiated significant change. They have managed to do this by setting up a contract or agreement which mimics the outside

Are clear about the business they are in

Invest in PR and in Product Development

Manage their internal boundaries well

Have a champion at board level

Relate their activities to the organization's strategy

Say 'No' to low priority work

Network outside their organization

Take a business approach to costs

Deliver more than clients expect

Have presence

Behave a little differently, but not too differently!

Turn client needs into wants (with strategic connections)

Are confident they measure up to external consultants

Figure 27 Successful internal consultancies

consultant's practice in negotiating a contract. This formalises their role in a particular project, and they can set clear objectives and processes. They can also allow a little distance between that part of the organization they are working with, and develop a closeness between the client and the change agent. When change agents are internal to the system, it is desirable for them to contract formally with the client in a very similar way to the external consultant. They should also be confident that they have the freedom to refuse an assignment. Figure 27 shows a list of characteristics that the author has developed while working with a number of internal change agents and consultancies.

3. Employee as change agent

Currently, many readers will not have adopted the change agent role, but some may be wondering how they can use change technology within their own managerial work, and indeed may have been members of standard-setting groups and see this as a framework, providing some leverage for change. Lancaster and Lancaster[1] provide a readable text which describes the role (in the US) of the nurse as an internal change agent. They see internal change as a basic management responsibility. They see a change agent as someone who demonstrates goal-seeking behaviour, with a clear logical sequence of actions, as someone who is responsible for:

- stimulation of ideas; diagnosis of need or problem
- assessment of motivation and resources for the change effort
- assessment of capability to change
- diagnosis of the type of change needed
- development of the implementation strategy
- trying out the implementation strategy
- revision of strategies
- implementation
- observation, handling, avoidance of or overcoming resistance to the project
- evaluation of the effectiveness of the change
- formulation of recommendations for future action or modifications.

However, their emphasis is rather more with managing and mobilizing others, and *imposing change*: 'Once the goals are established and resources and hindrances are identified, the change agent can begin to delegate and assign responsibility to participants.'

Each internal change agent has to develop his or her own style. But the preference in this book is towards a more *enabling* approach, so the organization is left more empowered to cope with change, after the intervention. However, each change agent has to find a style that fits their internal status and preferences, and yet is still effective. It may be that working for change in your own post can more usefully involve rather more expert input or more prescriptive methods, but the principles of change will, of course, be just the same.

Change Project: An Example

The following case study demonstrates an unplanned change project, arising from changed external demands on the service, using an internal change agent.

Demands are changing in genito-urinary (GU) medicine (known to most as VD clinics), primarily because of the increase in HIV infection and the fear of this infection, and the higher expectations of consumers. In one clinic, this had resulted in an increase of complaints to management and disruptions in the clinic from dissatisfied customers. Many of the staff were aware of the changing demands and wanted to change their practice to modify the service they provided. Some staff felt a change in policy was needed: they felt they should be dealing with 'high risk groups' separately and holding preventive educational sessions. They thought it would be effective but costly, requiring an investment in training, an increase in staff and a rescheduling of existing staff.

The Business manager was keen to work on the change problem in a well-structured way, and not to be led simply into paying the bills for increased staff and expensive training courses that these changes seemed to necessitate. He wanted a planned service. Because of this, he was refusing to pay for the huge cartons of condoms that were blocking the clinic, until the matter had been properly reviewed. These condoms became a matter of some significance since they reflected the basic differences in key people's view of the 'business' (or mission) of the department. Was it preventive or curative? An outside change consultant was called in to help with the initial diagnosis.

1. Defining the current state

Environmental mapping with key people demonstrated a complex system with many boundary issues (see Figure 28) which would need addressing in any change process. The demands on the clinic had recently changed, but the services had not. Internally, there was no culture of change or innovation to encourage such changes of response.

Individual, structured interviews (X) were held with a

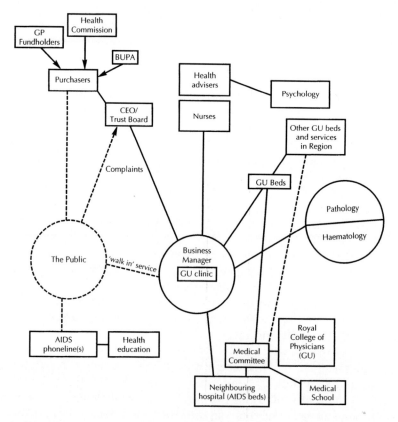

Figure 28 GU clinic: current system

transverse slice of the workforce in the clinic and from the boundaries. Figure 29 portrays a transverse slice. Individuals from different levels in the structure were selected to represent the widest range of roles and responsibilities from the 'bottom' to the 'top'.

Each of the staff completed the 'health of the organization questionnaire' (Appendix B). The analysis of this and the individual interviews revealed:

● a low level of internal cohesion – information was not being widely shared. There were good informal relationships between staff;

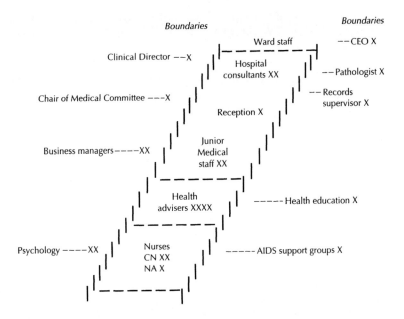

Figure 29 Transverse slice of workforce in GU clinic

- the clinic had a low level of creative thinking and cultural problem-solving;
- the clinic had confused 'mission', policy-making and policy implementation;
- the clinic had poor information systems. Although some junior individuals were initiating their own monitoring systems, these were done mostly in isolation;
- staff development was occurring within discipline, but was not closely related to the department's 'mission';
- poor relationships with purchasers.

A lack of cross-professional communication is generally seen in organizations that are low in innovation.[2]

Overall it appeared that there were some good new ideas from individuals, particularly at the shop-floor level, but there was some difficulty in bringing these ideas to fruition. Certain ideas were identified:

- 'We could save minutes off each attendance if we extended the nursing role.'

- 'If we could even up the patient flow, we would reduce waiting time.' A mixed appointment and walk-in system was suggested.
- Information systems: 'Apparently, we are not doing the same amount of work we did a year ago with half the number of doctors. Perhaps the cases have changed? We don't know enough about our case mix to make the best use of time or staff.'
- Reviewing pathology tests: 'Why do we do so many? It's very costly and some tests are not even related to VD.'

This information was shared, first, with those staff who had contributed and then with other key people, both in and on the boundaries of the GU clinic. It was agreed that those with the ideas on change (the shop-floor staff) should be given assistance to bring their ideas to fruition.

2. Describe future state

A project group was formed, consisting of the key people. This group began to define the desired future for the clinic to drive the changes through.

3. Present to future state analysis

3.1 Readiness and capability

This was estimated (see Table 2). It listed the key people and their readiness and capability for the proposed changes (X represents current level and O the potential level). If capability was low, less time would be spent in working with the individual. In other words, if someone has no further potential as a resource to the change effort, then it is *less* efficient to spend time with someone *less* capable of helping (see reverse score of Business manager). This showed where the effort should be directed.

3.2 Forcefield analysis

This was compiled from an analysis of the key people and showed where some of the difficulties were (see Figure 30).

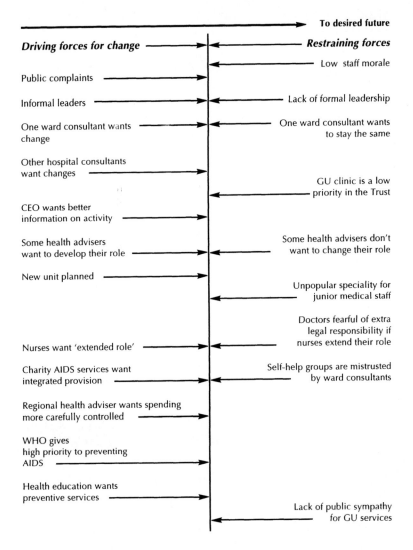

To desired future

Driving forces for change ──────▶ ◀── *Restraining forces*

◀── Low staff morale

Public complaints ──────▶

Informal leaders ──────▶ ◀── Lack of formal leadership

One ward consultant wants ──────▶ ◀── One ward consultant wants
change   to stay the same

Other hospital consultants
want changes ──────▶

                                        GU clinic is a low
                        ◀── priority in the Trust

CEO wants better
information on activity ──────▶

Some health advisers   Some health advisers don't
want to develop their role ──────▶ ◀── want to change their role

New unit planned ──────▶

                                        Unpopular speciality for
                        ◀── junior medical staff

                                        Doctors fearful of extra
                                        legal responsibility if
Nurses want 'extended role' ──────▶ ◀── nurses extend their role

Charity AIDS services want   Self-help groups are mistrusted
integrated provision ──────▶ ◀── by ward consultants

Regional health adviser wants spending
more carefully controlled ──────▶

WHO gives
high priority to preventing
AIDS ──────▶

Health education wants
preventive services ──────▶

                                        Lack of public sympathy
                        ◀── for GU services

Figure 30 GU clinic: forcefield analysis

For instance, some individuals were pushing for change, but they were not very good at formulating ways of making the changes.

Table 2 GU clinic: readiness/capability charting from the client's charting

Key players	Readiness			Capability		
	High	Medium	Low	High	Medium	Low
Doctor 1	O —— X			OX		
Doctor 2	OX			OX		
Doctor 3		O —— X		O ————————— X		
Business manager	X —— O				OX	
Nurse manager	OX				OX	
Community nurse 1	O ——————— X			O —— X		
Community nurse 2	O —— X				OX	
Health adviser 1		OX				OX
Health adviser 2	O —— X				OX	
Health adviser 3	O —— X			OX		
Psychologist	O —— X				OX	
Records officer	O —— X			O —— X		
Reception 1	O ——————— X			OX		
Reception 2	O ——————— X			OX		

X = Current level
O = Potential level

3.3 Change equation

This is really a shorthand way of indicating the three areas in which to apply the pressure:

(1) building up a vision of the future that people want;
(2) making them dissatisfied with current performance;
(3) showing that it is easy to change by designing the first steps.

But (1) × (2) × (3) must be greater than the cost of change, which is usually high.

All readers will be aware of the difficulty involved in making any changes in large organizations. It often seems easier to continue to do things the same way. The change agent therefore has to be skilled in using 'levers' to make the organization realize that changes are preferable to standing still. The change equation outlines the areas of focus that can create dissonance and upset the current state, and push organization into feeling change is less costly than staying the same.

3.4 Summary of 'leverage'

In the GU clinic, it was clear that there was increasing interest an a different 'future'. In particular, those staff in close contact with the public felt that things could improve. They knew things could be done better. As they gathered support for change, they encouraged the idea that the service need not stay the same. They used their strong informal friendships to gather support for these views and extend it to other staff. This had the effect of seemingly making the 'cost of change' decrease.

The forcefield analysis (see Figure 30) had shown that many forces were working for change (on the left). These became more obvious during the project group meetings. A top priority was seen as a new mission statement. They tried out the following wording: 'A clinic selling preventative and treatment services for those with, or at risk of, sexually transmitted diseases.'

Once the mission was agreed, the steering group saw the need to negotiate with related services (their boundaries). If they were to become more involved in preventative approaches, they needed to involve other groups and staff, such as the health education department, the local authority education department, medical school and nursing staff, and so on, and to have patients prepared accurately by GPs for their visit to the clinic. Fairly informal arrangements already existed with AIDS services and local high risk groups, like the gay community, but these links had to become much more efficient and a recognised part of a new preventative service. This meant some work on negotiating with boundary agencies that already existed and improving communications to help the unit work to its 'new' mission.

4. Define work to be done

Remember how economical it can be to find one area that needs changing which automatically reduces work at other pressure points? For instance, rescheduling an HIV clinic (where each individual needing more time is allocated to a particular session in the week) might reduce the long waiting time for other patients who have just dropped in for some swift check-up. If it provided in-depth counselling skills part time and, therefore more economically, this could lead to a reduction in the number of complaints received from AIDS patients who needed highly skilled counselling. It was also expected to reduce the complaints and violence from frustrated attenders, who had a long wait.

In checking which areas to begin with, and looking for possible domino effects, the clinic focused on:

- policies
- working procedures
- control and information systems
- training methods.

In the clinic, the first emphasis was on improving information systems. Some of the ward staff were already collecting their own limited information, since they were unsure what was happening and wanted to know how well their bit of the service was doing. The Business manager was unsure of the overall performance of the ward and how much it all cost, so contracting was a big problem for him.

Once together in the project group, the staff expressed their increasing concern that they had no check on performance or efficiency, and on ways of monitoring improvements in their own practice. Ward staff also demanded systems that could give more information in current performance. This perceived need for information became a corner stone for the transition plan. The staff also recognised that better communications were needed between ward staff, the boundary groups and key individuals.

Once better formal communications were developed, other key issues had a clearer route to follow. For example, discussions with the pathology department on appropriate types of testing became much easier to initiate once the channels of communication were open for policies to be developed, agreed and monitored.

5. Transition planning

There were particular difficulties for this group when managing the transition state.

1. Referring back to the section on resistance to change (see Chapter 2), the reader will remember the dual focus on:

   (a) the individual's security level;
   (b) the organization's tolerance for change.

   Many individuals were not keen on change and found the ideas highly threatening. The organization was similarly not used to innovation to change.

2. Also, many projects flounder because transitions need more resources. Keeping the current 'show in the road', as well as developing new ways of working, can be personally draining and costly in human and financial resources. In the GU clinic, unchanged day-to-day services had to be managed alongside new practices (for example, the new HIV work).

3. Both formal and informal systems were changing with some loosening of traditional practices. This unfreezing stage also allowed leadership potential in existing staff to be identified and encouraged. Specific tasks were agreed at the project group, as shown in Table 3 (see Chapter 2).

In summary, the clinic had begun to work out its own solutions to an external pressure, and to use its human resources, its skilled staff, in new ways. The emphasis was more in developing processes and systems that gave information, and allowed appraisal and review, so the service could change and renew as external conditions changed.

Table 3 Task analysis for transitions

Task	Doctors 1	2	3	Business manager	Receptionist	CEO	Psychologist	Project leader
Gather information on current waiting time	I	I	I	I	R	I	O	S
Set up HIV clinic	R	S	S	S	S	I	O	S
Arrange counselling training course for:								
Doctors	S	S	R	I	O	S	R	I
Health advisers	I	I	I	S	O	S	R	I
Set up weekly ward meetings	S	S	S	S	S	I	I	R

I = informed; R = responsible; S = Support; O = no role.

References

1. Lancaster, J., and W. Lancaster, *The Nurse as a Change Agent* (Mosby, 1982).
2. Kanter, R. M., *The Change Masters* (Allen & Unwin, 1984).

Chapter 5 Identifying Training and Development Needs

Management Style

Knowing more about yourself, your range of skills, the way you prefer to function both interpersonally and in teams, is essential in managing change and getting the best from the people you manage. This chapter includes exercises designed to help you assess your own behavioural style, and to give you an opportunity to develop a wider range of style. They might best be done as part of training or during 'time-out' with your own team.

Exercise 7: Management style

Consider the vexed question of parking spaces. You have three priority spaces to be allocated to the 24 staff of a day hospital for the elderly. You have managerial charge of this team and your brief is to give management an answer as soon as possible. Whose names are to be put on the three spaces? (Remember this exercise is intended to increase your flexibility of response.)

To do this exercise, you have to get all the team together and tackle the issue in a variety of styles.

1. Tell them what you have decided (*autocratic*).
2. List the rational arguments and, after discussion, take a vote for the best option (*rationalist*).
3. Facilitate the discussion around certain agreed key issues, letting feelings be displayed and the preferred team option emerge (*facilitator*).

These three styles may not all be as easy for you as each other. See which preferred style you adopt immediately and then try the others in turn. Invite feedback from the other team members on how they felt with your preferred styles, then adopt your *less*-preferred styles.

This exercise can be undertaken with a group of managers of the same level playing roles, or a multi-disciplinary team. The best outcome can be achieved if leaders choose to swop management styles and follow the rules for feedback given later in this chapter (p. 106).

This exercise is one simple example, very briefly described, which can be used to estimate and develop your own management styles. Many other exercises exist (see Margerison[1] and MCB University Press[2]), which can be useful in extending your repertoire.

The Self-assessment Tool

The self-assessment tool has been developed for managers in the Health Service so that they can learn about themselves and the way they are perceived by other people (see Exercise 8). It uses self-appraisal, as well as peer and 'boss' appraisal. It provides a rich way in which to develop your own plans to get the wide range of skills you need for different occasions and for various demands. Having a wide range of skills in your repertoire will give you greater flexibility and control, and a better chance to take advantage of change opportunities.

The tool is designed to be used by:

1. yourself and ideal self (as self-assessment)
2. peers (about you)
3. your boss (about you)
4. subordinates (about you).

1. Yourself

Rate *yourself* on the items listed, then rate your *ideal self*. This will give you the levels you feel you can aspire to, and it will also provide a *discrepancy* score; that is, the difference between your current self and your ideal self. This gives you a realistic appraisal of what you are aiming at and what you want to work on.

2. Peers

Invite a colleague you trust, and who knows you and your performance reasonably well, to fill in the schedule for you. Make it clear at the outset how you plan to use the results. You could suggest that you will discuss it later with your colleague, or you could suggest that you will be taking it away and will never mention it again! This should be agreed at the outlet.

If you choose someone whose opinion you don't value, the results will be rejectable, and you will be in danger of selecting only those results you wish to hear!

3. Boss

This is tricky in an era of performance review and staff appraisal. However, there is good evidence that performance varies with situations and relationships, so getting the widest range of perceptions about your personal performance and skill will demonstrate to you the range of behaviours at your own disposal. It may also demonstrate that you are under-using some skills in certain relationships. For instance, it may be easier for you to express strong feelings with subordinates, but you may find it harder to do it with your boss. However, a genuine demonstration that this really matters to you could be useful in making a case to your boss.

4. Subordinates

This is another tricky area. You will need to consider how this exercise will be viewed by your subordinates. This will mean discussing the reasons for doing it quite clearly and openly before you ask them to help by filling in the schedule. With some subordinates, it may be seen as an opportunity to 'curry favour' or to 'settle old scores'. Either way, the assessment may be difficult for you to use. As with the boss, it is essential to decide beforehand how much you will value the results you have invited.

5. The process of getting feedback

It may be useful here to outline some rules for feedback. Ground-rules about the process of giving and receiving feedback about yourself could be structured by giving each of your assessors the following list. This could become part of the contract to help you, and would indeed control the kind of content that is given back to you, and could maximize its usefulness. It may also reassure your colleagues about your reactions to their ratings of you!

The giver should:
- be specific–*not* general
- be considerate and helpful – bad feedback can be damaging
- address behaviours that *can* be changed – not unchangeables (for example, 'You're too tall'.)
- give feedback as soon as you can – it is more effective in changing behaviour
- check with the receiver – ensure he or she understands the message
- be descriptive – not evaluative
- Say, for example, 'You made me feel unsettled' – not 'You unsettle everyone.'

Remember: Feedback is given for the *receiver's* benefit – not the *giver's*!

As receiver you should:
- only ask for feedback you want
- only ask people you trust, otherwise it's rejectable if you don't like it
- ask for clarification if you don't understand
- avoid arguing, justifying, denying
- make your own choice about what to do with the information (ponder, accept, seek more information)

Exercise 8: Self-assessment of management skills

The aim of this inventory is to help you learn more about your managerial performance from people around you. You might like to fill it in for yourself, your ideal self, then ask your boss, a peer and a subordinate, but only if you feel that they will be helpful and truthful in their scoring. (0 indicates never true and 5 always true.
Circle the appropriate number.) There is space to add your own items.

Self   *Name*

(1)	Evaluates and changes own performance	0	1	2	3	4	5
(2)	Tolerates conflict	0	1	2	3	4	5
(3)	Describes own values clearly	0	1	2	3	4	5
(4)	Can express strong feelings	0	1	2	3	4	5
(5)	Handles criticism	0	1	2	3	4	5
(6)	Can reflect opinion	0	1	2	3	4	5
(7)	Can reflect feelings	0	1	2	3	4	5
(8)	Manages own stress	0	1	2	3	4	5
(9)	Effectively manages time	0	1	2	3	4	5
(10)	Knows own strengths and weaknesses	0	1	2	3	4	5
(11)	Adapts personal style to fit the situation	0	1	2	3	4	5
(12)	Receives feedback constructively	0	1	2	3	4	5
(13)	Actively learns from everyday experience	0	1	2	3	4	5
(14)	Recognizes the stress in own life	0	1	2	3	4	5
(15)	Manages own strengths and weaknesses well	0	1	2	3	4	5
(16)	Can energise others	0	1	2	3	4	5
(17)	Has the ability to make others feel good about themselves	0	1	2	3	4	5
(18)	Transmits own values, in a clear and simple manner	0	1	2	3	4	5
(19)	Processes data rapidly	0	1	2	3	4	5
(20)	Copes with uncertainty and dilemma	0	1	2	3	4	5
(21)	Can conceptualise in abstract terms	0	1	2	3	4	5
(22)	Can translate principle into practice	0	1	2	3	4	5
(23)	Can take a 'helicopter' objective view	0	1	2	3	4	5
(24)	Welcomes challenge	0	1	2	3	4	5
(25)	Has positive self-regard	0	1	2	3	4	5
(26)	Can engender leadership in others	0	1	2	3	4	5
(27)		0	1	2	3	4	5
(28)		0	1	2	3	4	5

Self and others

(1)	Relates well to staff ar all levels	0	1	2	3	4	5
(2)	Is sensitive to others' values	0	1	2	3	4	5
(3)	Uses appropriate listening/talking balance	0	1	2	3	4	5

(4)	Understands underlying group processes	0	1	2	3	4	5
(5)	Is influenced by others	0	1	2	3	4	5
(6)	Can gain group support	0	1	2	3	4	5
(7)	Can motivate a group	0	1	2	3	4	5
(8)	Uses confrontation constructively	0	1	2	3	4	5
(9)	Negotiates constructively between competing views	0	1	2	3	4	5
(10)	Listens actively	0	1	2	3	4	5
(11)	Instructs clearly	0	1	2	3	4	5
(12)	Recognises others' feeling accurately	0	1	2	3	4	5
(13)	Can sell ideas	0	1	2	3	4	5
(14)	Builds on the contribution of others	0	1	2	3	4	5
(15)	Can clarify unstructured group ideas	0	1	2	3	4	5
(16)	Handles group conflict constructively	0	1	2	3	4	5
(17)	Can encourage appropriate participation	0	1	2	3	4	5
(18)	Can keep a group 'on task'	0	1	2	3	4	5
(19)	Can close a group effectively	0	1	2	3	4	5
(20)	Gives feedback constructively	0	1	2	3	4	5
(21)	Demands excellence of self and others	0	1	2	3	4	5
(22)	Can convey meaning in a simple way	0	1	2	3	4	5
(23)	Discriminates between the essential and the desirable	0	1	2	3	4	5
(24)	Delegates clearly	0	1	2	3	4	5
(25)	Readily takes decisions	0	1	2	3	4	5
(26)	Is good at managing change	0	1	2	3	4	5
(27)		0	1	2	3	4	5
(28)		0	1	2	3	4	5

Self and organization

(1)	Has the ability to get speedily to the heart of the matter	0	1	2	3	4	5
(2)	Uses resources imaginatively	0	1	2	3	4	5
(3)	Identifies the critical factors impacting on him/her	0	1	2	3	4	5
(4)	Creates a common vision with those around	0	1	2	3	4	5
(5)		0	1	2	3	4	5
(6)		0	1	2	3	4	5

Ratings by:

Summary sheets

	Self	Ideal self	Boss	Peer 1	Peer 2	Subordinate
Summary of self						
(1) Evaluates and changes own performance						
(2) Tolerates conflict						
(3) Describes own values clearly						
(4) Can express strong feelings						
(5) Handles criticism						
(6) Can reflect opinion						
(7) Can reflect feelings						
(8) Manages own stress						
(9) Effectively manages time						
(10) Knows own strengths and weaknesses						
(11) Adapts personal style to fit the situation						
(12) Receives feedback constructively						
(13) Actively learns from everyday experience						
(14) Recognizes the stress in own life						
(15) Manages own strengths and weaknesses well						
(16) Can energize others						
(17) Has the ability to make others feel good about themselves						
(18) Transmits own values, in a clear and simple manner						
(19) Processes data rapidly						
(20) Copes with uncertainty and dilemma						
(21) Can conceptualize in abstract terms						
(22) Can translate principle into practice						
(23) Can take a 'helicopter' objective view						
(24) Welcomes challenge						
(25) Has positive self-regard						
(26) Can engender leadership in others						
(27)						
(28)						

	Self	Ideal self	Boss	Peer 1	Peer 2	Subordinate
Summary of self and others						
(1) Relates well to staff at all levels						
(2) Is sensitive to others' values						
(3) Uses appropriate listening/talking balance						
(4) Understands underlying group processes						
(5) Is influenced by others						
(6) Can gain group support						
(7) Can motivate a group						
(8) Uses confrontation constructively						

(9) Negotiates constructively between
     competing views
(10) Listens actively
(11) Instructs clearly
(12) Recognises others' feelings accurately
(13) Can sell ideas
(14) Builds on the contribution of others
(15) Can clarify unstructured group ideas
(16) Handles group conflict constructively
(17) Can encourage appropriate participation
(18) Can keep a group 'on task'
(19) Can close a group effectively
(20) Gives feedback constructively
(21) Demands excellence of self and others
(22) Can convey meaning in a simple way
(23) Discriminates between the essential and
     the desirable
(24) Delegates clearly
(25) Readily takes decisions
(26) Is good at managing change
(27)
(28)

Summary of self and organization
 (1) Has the ability to get speedily to the
     heart of the matter
 (2) Uses resources imaginatively
 (3) Identifies the critical factors impacting
     on him/her
 (4) Creates a common vision with those
     around
 (5)
 (6)

6. Results

The results from your evaluation can be gathered on the summary sheets provided. You can enter the rater's name and/or position at the top and list their scores. Then it is easy to scan the high and low points of your scores and to note the discrepancies.

You may find that your own scores do not match others'

view of you, and possibly might be closer to your own *ideal*. This will give you some ideas on your own development and training needs, but it may also suggest certain skills you have but don't use commonly, or might be useful more often or in different situations.

A management skills checklist might be useful now (see Exercise 9). This personal checklist allows you, firstly, to score the skills that are important to your job and, secondly, to highlight how good you are in these skills. Knowing your deficits and your strengths is a good way of understanding which ones you are naturally good at, and making a case to your senior officers for further training! Also, it can help to select people around you who complement your own skills. These kind of assessments are also useful in giving confidence about your diversity of skills.

Exercise 9: Management skills checklist

There are many skills that managers need to perform effectively in their jobs. This exercise presents a list of the most common skills, although not all jobs will demand them. Which skills are important in your job? How well developed are your skills in each area? Which do you feel you need extra opportunities to develop? Score your skills on a scale of 0–10.

Skill	Importance in job	How good at
(1) Motivating people to do things		
(2) Building a good team		
(3) Communicating well		
(4) Handling grievances		
(5) Disciplining subordinates		
(6) Chairing or conducting meetings		
(7) Briefing people		
(8) Interviewing		
(9) Getting on with other people		
(10) Leading a group		
(11) Persuading and influencing other people		
(12) Managing your time		
(13) Assessing yourself		
(14) Making presentations		

111

(15)	Writing reports	
(16)	Making decisions	
(17)	Planning work	
(18)	Setting targets/goals	
(19)	Organizing people and tasks	
(20)	Analyzing and diagnosing problems	
(21)	Designing and implementing procedures or systems	
(22)	Delegating	
(23)	Allocating work	
(24)	Assessing job performance of others	
(25)	Counselling and developing subordinates	
(26)	Writing job descriptions	
(27)	Costing and other financial matters	
(28)	Developing own technical job skills	

When you have rated each skill for both aspects (importance and how good you are at them), look back and identify those with the biggest difference between the two rating scores – that is, high on importance, but low on 'good at'. These are your key development needs.

Management Arenas

It might be useful at this stage to suggest that, rather than develop *all* the skills your job requires, you might consider the potent effect of networking. Kotter and Lawrence[3] in their study of US mayors showed that, although an individual's tasks and skills can be wide-ranging and strong, at times the network can compensate for deficits in certain areas (see Figure 31). This will depend on the agenda item that's being worked and the domain or area of operation that's being undertaken. Some examples might demonstrate how a good manager can compensate for deficits in his or her own skills.

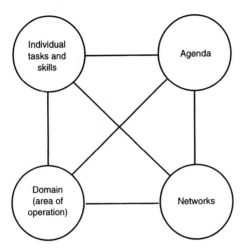

Figure 31 Management arenas (loosely based on Kotter and Lawrence, *Mayors in Actions,* Wiley, 1974)

Case study 10

If a ward manager finds public speaking difficult, he or she may either choose to train up that skill, in order to promote the ward's successes, or choose to network and find someone close who is a good public speaker.

In one hospice, the chief executive fostered his second-in-line who was an outgoing ambitious young man, very skilled in public presentation. The two used each other for their complementary skills; the chief executive helped the younger man with his career, while the second-in-line promoted the image of the hospice for fundraising on public platforms. If it is not always possible to develop the full range of skills yourself, networking can compensate.

Check Exercise 9 and Figure 31 and note your own individual skills for certain different areas of operation. Check off any areas where networking may be advised for the different agendas and domains.

1. Group assessment

In any group, people will adopt different roles at different times, according to the task and their preference, although some roles will more commonly be adopted by some people than others. Belbin's Situational Management Questionnaire[4] has been widely used for group performance and identifies the most powerful roles in a team (see Figure 32).

This tool is recommended for readers to study in more depth. It must be obvious that too much duplication of roles could be dysfunctional in a team. For instance, two completers could spend their time arguing over detail; too many company workers can have a stultifying effect.

It is particularly important in building new teams which are to steer an organization through change that people with complementary types of roles are chosen. If they are not, and new roles need developing, it is important to give training and reorientation opportunities, so they could, if they wished, develop their second most preferred role.

Women in Management

Because of the high proportion of women in nursing, this section is included partly to help managers develop the female potential in their workforce, but also to share the particular pressures women undoubtedly experience.

Few women attain top management jobs, but the Opportunity 2000 initiative is at least setting new targets and helping with training and so on. Women students feel it a distinct disadvantage being a woman if they want a job in management.[5]

A number of reasons for this low proportion have been postulated. These include the possibility that the value systems of current management are built on male attributes, which are not the values that women share, and so they simply don't apply for top jobs. But it has also been suggested that some women simply are not given appropriate career development opportunities, are given less risky projects.

Work has been done with groups of women to examine their

Type	Symbol	Typical features	Positive qualities	Allowable weaknesses
Company worker	CW	Conservative, dutiful, predictable	Organizing ability, practical, common sense, hard working, self-discipline	Lack of flexibility, unresponsiveness to unproven ideas
Coordinator	CO	Calm, self-confident, controlled	A capacity for treating and welcoming all potential contributors on their merits and without prejudice	No more than ordinary in terms of intellect or creative ability
Shaper	SH	Highly strung outgoing, dynamic	Drive and readiness to challenge inertia, ineffectiveness, complacency or self-deception	Proneness to provocation, irritation, and impatience
Plant	PL	Individualistic serious-minded unorthodox	Genius, imagination, intellect, knowledge	Up in the clouds, inclined to disregard practical details or protocol
Resource investigator	RI	Extroverted, enthusiastic, curious	A capacity for contacting people and exploring anything new. An ability to respond to challenge	Liable to lose interest once the initial fascination has passed
Monitor/Evaluator	ME	Sober, unemotional, prudent	Judgement, discretion hard-headedness	Lacks inspiration or the ability to motivate others
Team worker	TW	Socially orientated, rather mild, sensitive	An ability to respond to people and to situations and to promote team spirit	Indecisiveness at moments of crisis
Completer/finisher	CF	Painstakingly orderly conscientious, anxious	A capacity for follow-through Perfectionism	A tendency to worry about small things. A reluctance to 'let go'

Figure 32 Roles – based on Belbin

views of management and to see how congruent they were with the current managerial models. The models they developed for themselves as more acceptable, suggested a more 'nurturing' style, using words like 'caring, compromise, valuing others'. They used less of the 'telling and directing', which were descriptive words they found when working with mixed groups of managers, and which are found in most training textbooks[6] – leadership, motivation, communication, interaction, decision making, goal setting, control and performance. Women are also less likely to get credit for good work – see Tannen.[7]

As stated earlier, this section has been included to highlight the particular needs of organizations to develop the potential in their women staff, but also for women managers reading this book to feel reassured that it is well recognized that their role is not easy, and the strain is shared by many other women managers.

Cooper and Davidson[8] specify the problems and pressures that they isolated as 'specific to women managers':

- burdens of coping with the role of being the 'token' woman
- lack of role models
- a feeling of isolation
- strains of coping with prejudice and sex stereotyping
- overt and indirect discrimination from fellow employees, employers, and the organizational structure and climate.

Of the stresses 'intrinsic to the job', they found:

- work overload
- feeling undervalued
- 'being the boss'
- having to acquire male managerial skills
- being unable to attend training away from home.

It is interesting to note that this research found that successful women managers showed all the abilities and skills of their male counterparts, and indeed in some studies some were somewhat superior. This may simply confirm the view that successful women managers have adopted male values and performance, and have succeeded by fitting in. Indeed, male role models are usually the predominating ones in our successful organizations, so it is difficult for women to learn from other successful females and build up managerial skills that might fit their preferences better. One particular problem relates to successful women being described as both assertive or pushy.

Research on conversation shows that women do not generally get as much 'air time' as men, and women who do interrupt and insist on 'air time' equivalent to men are seen as persistent, tenacious and annoying by their male colleagues. One woman described her high profile work as an executive as 'walking a tightrope'. She felt that colleagues, observers and subordinates were simply waiting for her to make a mistake and fall.

At a recent workshop with a group of middle and senior women managers from a psychiatric hospital, some of the conclusions were highly congruent with this research, and it seemed worth summarising their conclusions here, simply to demonstrate how women can help themselves to develop their potential more fully in what, to many female readers, must appear to be a hostile managerial environment.

Case study 11: Women managers' group

The group consisted of mainly middle and senior managers working in a psychiatric hospital. They met for some months and had concentrated mainly on practical issues, like developing a crèche and a more sympathetic shift system. The issues that were raised at this event concerned:

- isolation and the need to network: As women were in a minority in senior managerial positions, it was seen as essential to develop mutual support and role models;
- assertion and confidence: displaying a confident persona meant demonstrating exactly where you stood and making that clear to others;
- ambition: 'If I'm happy, why incur the pain of going any further?'
- me at work, me at home: there seemed to be a strong *conflict* of roles and a need to resolve the tension between the demands of home and work;
- manager role versus carer role: this might have been specific to the psychiatric situation. Many of the senior managers had come up through the caring professions and found that 'the cut-throat, knife-edge' management style created conflict for them;
- emotional expression: learning to *handle* conflict without being accused of being a 'neurotic woman'!

It might be interesting to note a selection of individual action plans after this workshop:

● 'I need to manage stressful situation better, to deal with emotion and to find an acceptable way of dealing with conflict.'
● 'I need to be self-assured, to communicate clear messages about exactly where I stand.'
● 'I need to plan a clear career path and get a champion.'

Cooper and Davidson[9] provide a summary of guidance for women managers which may not apply to all women readers, but nevertheless makes useful reading.

● *Establish your priorities:* this will involve negotiating home and work, particularly if the woman's career must take precedence and mobility for the rest of the family is required.
● *Be assertive and speak up:* learn to say 'No' and avoid self-effacing behavior.
● *Take risks, but learn from your mistakes:* this may counteract the normal stereotype of women as more cautious.
● *Maintain career visibility:* be seen at the right committees and engage in the right activities.
● *Focus on the relevant:* don't just keep busy, but do those jobs central to your role plus those that will be noticed by top management.
● *Be strong:* have the courage and confidence to do what you think is right, regardless of the pressures.
● *Look out for yourself:* keep politically aware – watch your back!
● *Help other women:* not only will this give you mutual support with the same kind of problems, but in the long run it will develop an 'old girl network' which could challenge the old boy network for successful career development and recruitment.

Women are not reaching the senior management positions they are capable of. This appears to be partly due to a reluctance to fit into 'male' value systems, but it is also related to the general social disadvantages of being a woman, like maintaining home responsibilities alongside work pressures.

References

1. Margerison, C., *How to Assess Your Managerial Style* (MCB Press, 1979).
2. MCB University Press Ltd, 62 Toller Lane, Bradford, Yorks.
3. Kotter, J. and P. R. Lawrence, *Mayors in Action* (Wiley, 1974).
4. Belbin, R.M., *Management Teams – Why They Succeed or Fail* (Heinemann, 1981).
5. Cooper, C. and M. Davidson, *High Pressure: Working Lives of Women Managers* (Fontana, 1982).
6. Lickert, R., *New Patterns of Management* (McGraw-Hill Kogakusha Ltd, 1961).
7. Tannen, D., 'The Power of Talk', *Harvard Business Review*, **73** (5) 138–48.
8. Cooper and Davidson, *High Pressure*.
9. Ibid.

Appendix A   Managing Your Own Change Project

The following exercise is included here to bring together all the steps you will need in following your change project.

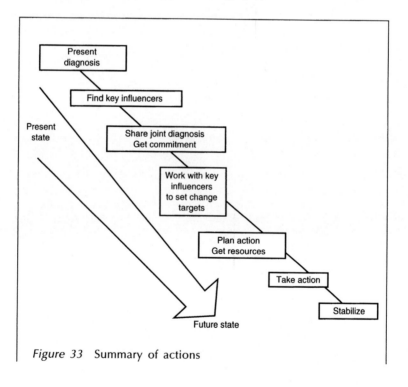

Figure 33   Summary of actions

1. *Open system analysis: Identifying your current management concerns/issues*

   (a) Are you happy with your own role?
   (b) Do you need further assessment/training/role modification? (See 'Role Effectiveness Profile' in Appendix C.)
   (c) Are you happy with your unit's performance?
   (d) What is the unit's mission?
   (e) What are the various demands on the unit?
   (f) What are the various unit responses to these demands?
   (g) What are the unmet demands?
   (h) What are the boundary systems? Identify key people and key domains (environmental mapping).
   (i) Do you manage these systems well?
   (j) What are the strengths and weaknesses in your unit? It may help to look at all the arenas (individuals, tasks, formal organization, informal organization).
   (k) What is the culture of change? Should this be increased or decreased?
   (l) What happens if your unit doesn't change? Describe what things will look like if you do nothing.

2. *Defining the future*

   (a) Check against your environmental map and taking your key domains ask:

      • What demand do you want it/them to be making on your unit?
      • What responses would you like to be making?

   (b) Compose future scenarios as if you were taking a helicopter view. What would look different? (Take a future view that seems attainable, not one that is too far away.)

3. *What changes are needed?*

   These changes should be clearer if you compare your present with your future. Are these changes in: attitudes, behaviours, policies, methods?

4. *Forcefield analysis*

   (a) What are the forces for and against change? (Which forces against can you work with?)
   (b) What do you yourself bring to this change effort? (power, influence, formal and informal role)
   (c) What are the various reasons for wanting change?
   (d) Where should you target your efforts?
   (e) Who and what is vulnerable to change?
   (f) Where is the best place to start? (Remember the domino effect. If you start with one of the problems, will others fall into place more easily?)

- You can now look at the desired change you want to make:

  Driving for desired change   *Restraining for desired change*

  ───────────────────▶   ◀───────────────────
  ───────────────────▶   ◀───────────────────

  Personal
  Interpersonal   (Look at all of
  Group   these terms)
  Organizational

  (g) Have you included all the important variables?
  (h) Are there areas where you need more information? If you need more information, how are you going to get it?

5. *Environmental mapping*: this will have suggested where sources of help might be available. Identify 'key' people. You will need to build up key people's readiness and capability. List key people, and rate their readiness and capability.

key people/system	*Readiness*			*Capability*		
	H	M	L	H	M	L
_____	—	—	—	—	—	—
_____	—	—	—	—	—	—

6. *Readiness and capability*
   Ask of the key people:

   (a) How ready (high, medium, low) are the key people to change in the direction you want?
   (b) How capable (high, medium, low) are they at driving or helping the change? (This concerns power and influence, where influence generally means allocation of resources.)

7. *Self-assessment*

   (a) What do you bring to the change effort? (skill, influence, motives and motivation)
   (b) What is your current state and ability to energize the process?
   (c) Are you seen as influential by others?
   (d) Can you control rewards of others?
   (e) What are your reasons for this change?
   (f) How do others view your reasons?

Organizational reasons	*Versus*	*Personal reasons*
To improve efficiency, effectiveness or for unit to survive		To reduce pressure To have a quiet life To get promotion To impress professional peers

This balance must not be seen as too personally advantageous or you will be seen as personally pushy or empire building.

8. *Leverage: Building a desire for change*
   Remember the change equation. You have to address each lever point:

   (a) you can create dissatisfaction with the present performance
   (b) you can build up a shared vision of the future which is different
   (c) you can suggest some acceptable and easy-made first steps towards change.

   Which one have you chosen to start with? The costs are likely to be both organizational and individual. Remember to keep an optimal level of felt security in mind. The organization and the individual will be more ready to change if the level is neither too high nor too low. Levering too much will produce less security. You have a delicate balancing act between levering to create a more uncertain future and less security versus the tendency to retreat to the old and known.

9. *Transition*
   A transition plan should fit many possible scenarios, with a high level of uncertainty and instability for the participants. Are you prepared for the:

   Shock → Retreat → Acknowledgement → Adaptation

   stages, particularly the first two? What have you done to prepare others for these stages?

10. *Transition plans*
    What are your plans for managing:

    (a) The period of change? Are you building up a steering group, a project manager, a transition manager or what? Transitions need different structures and names
    (b) The unaffected parts of the system that are your responsibility?
    (c) The organizational integration of your unit during the change (for example, managing boundaries that will be affected by these transition plans)?
    (d) The future?

11. *Building commitment*

    (a) What is your plan for building commitment?
    (b) Which target individuals have you identified?
    (c) What is the critical mass (that is, the minimum number of people who will push this change through)? Develop a plan for getting the necessary commitment from this critical mass.

(d) What plans do you have for shifting key people from their present position (oppose, let, support, make) to the desired position?

12. *Responsibility for transition planning*

Take your critical mass and those people directly involved and see what kind of responsibility (responsible, support, inform) they should each have for each task. By breaking your tasks into subtasks, you can check which individual will be responsible and which you need approval from, and so on. Getting your group together to develop the chart is a way to develop good ownership at this stage. Each actor can check his or her responsibility and call the attention of other actors to any confusions there might be for who is taking responsibility for which part of the plan. Remember to minimize the numbers responsible for each task.

Your plan should be:

- purposeful
- task-specific
- integrated – the activities should be linked
- time-sequenced
- adaptable – things change!
- cost-effective.

13. *Evaluation*

(a) How are you planning to decide whether you have been successful in your change efforts?

(b) What are the transformations you were planning to make, and how will you know if you have made them?

14. *Boundaries*

(a) Who else does your critical mass and particularly yourself need to communicate with?

(b) Who else do you need to inform, instruct and persuade about the plans? Have you forgotten anyone?

Appendix B Health of the Organization Questionnaire

The following form lists 22 characteristics of an organization. First, on the scale of 1 to 8, rate your organization, as it is today, by putting crosses in the appropriate boxes. (NB: 'never true' to the left, 'always true' to the right)

Having completed the list, repeat the exercise, this time putting a tick in the box that, in your view, represents the ideal organization.

The difference between the tick and the cross, provides an indication of how far you see your organization from being healthy. The individual differences can be averaged to produce an overall rating. Where individuals place the marks on each scale will be very subjective but the value of the differences can be compared in a group. In this way it is possible to check the diagnosis of the need for change.

Are there some immediate actions that could be taken to improve things?

Are there any improvements which are especially important for the particular change programme being worked on?

	Never True								Always True	Difference
	1	2	3	4	5	6	7	8		
1. Consistent high-quality service is emphasized within the organization.										
2. The organization responds to the needs and views of its patients.										
3. The organization is well in touch with its environment, has its finger on the pulse of things.										

	Never True	1	2	3	4	5	6	7	8	Always True	Difference
4. The public see the organization as friendly.											
5. The organization's leaders create an exciting working environment through personal attention, persistence and direct intervention on every level.											
6. Managers are visible at all levels, they adopt a 'management by walkabout' approach.											
7. Staff know their managers well and what they 'stand for'.											
8. The organization has a well-defined, well-known set of guiding beliefs stated in qualitative terms.											
9. General objectives and values are set forth and widely shared throughout the organization.											
10. Information is widely shared – managers are open with their staff.											
11. Conflict is managed, not suppressed.											
12. The organization will try out new ideas and experiment without lengthy analysis and debate.											

	Never True								Always True	Difference
	1	2	3	4	5	6	7	8		
13. People are encouraged to be entrepreneurial, creative and innovative.										
14. Failure is seen as an opportunity to learn and a natural part of innovation and creativity.										
15. Managers assume that individuals want to take on more responsibility and provide opportunities for them to do so.										
16. An effort is made to inspire people at the very bottom of the organization.										
17. Management demonstrates respect for people and treat them as adults.										
18. People work effectively in multi-professional teams.										
19. Individuals are more concerned with contributing to the successful implementation of the task than defending personal or professional affairs.										
20. Casual, unstructured seemingly random yet task-related meetings frequently happen.										
21. The organization's form is simple, well-understood and easy to relate to what it is doing.										

Appendix B

	Never True									Always True	Difference
		1	2	3	4	5	6	7	8		
22. The organization is well-disciplined, tightly organized towards its key tasks yet provides and allows flexibility and freedom at the same time.											

How would you rate your organization in terms of effectiveness?

                                                                      Tick

One of the best, extremely effective   ☐

Better than many, very effective   ☐

OK, generally gets the job done   ☐

Effective in some areas, needs revamping in others   ☐

Marginally effective   ☐

(Source: E. A. Turrell, *Change and Innovation: A Challenge for the NHS*, The Institute of Health Services Management, 1986)

Appendix C   Role Effectiveness Profile – Tool for Self-Assessment

The purpose of this inventory is twofold:

1. to provide a structured way of thinking about your current role;
2. to enable positive action to be taken to improve your role effectiveness.

The more honest you attempt to be, the better the quality of data you will get back from this inventory. You will probably need to think carefully about the questions rather than make instant responses. Feel free to alter answers if you wish. It is *not* a psychological test.

Each question has three sets of statements which you might make about your current role. Tick the one which comes closest to describing your experience of your current role. You may choose only *one* statement in each set.

Tick

1. (a) My role is very important in this organization; I feel central here. (b) I am doing useful and fairly important work here. (c) Very little importance is given to my role in this organization; I feel peripheral here.	☐ ☐ ☐
2. (a) My training and expertise are not fully utilized in my present role. (b) My training and knowledge are not used in my present role. (c) I am able to use my knowledge and training very well here.	☐ ☐ ☐

3. (a) I have little freedom in my role;
I am only a messenger.
(b) I operate according to the direction
given to me.
(c) I can take initiative and act on my
own in my role.

4. (a) I am doing normal routine work in
my role.
(b) In my role I am able to use my
creativity and do something new.
(c) I have no time for creative work in
my role.

5. (a) No one in the organization
responds to my ideas and suggestions.
(b) I work in close collaboration with
some other colleagues.
(c) I am alone in my role and have
almost no one to consult.

6. (a) When I need some help none is available.
(b) Whenever I have a problem,
others help me.
(c) I get very hostile responses when
I ask for help.

7. (a) I do not have the opportunity to
contribute to society in my role.
(b) What I am doing in my role is
likely to help other organizations
or society at large.
(c) I have the opportunity to have
some effect on society at large.

8. (a) I make some contribution to decisions.
(b) I have no power here.
(c) My advice is accepted by my seniors.

9. (a) Some of what I do contributes to
my learning.
(b) I am slowly forgetting all that
I learned (my professional knowledge).
(c) I have tremendous opportunities
for professional growth in my role.

10. (a) I dislike being bothered with problems.

    (b) When a subordinate brings a problem to me, I help find a solution.

    (c) I refer the problem to my boss or to some other person.

11. (a) I feel quite central in the organization.

    (b) I think I am doing fairly important work.

    (c) My role is peripheral to the mainstream of the organization.

12. (a) I do not enjoy my role.

    (b) I enjoy my role very much.

    (c) I enjoy some parts of my role and not others.

13. (a) I have little freedom in my role.

    (b) I have a great deal of freedom in my role.

    (c) I have enough freedom in my role.

14. (a) I do a good job according to a schedule already decided.

    (b) I am able to be innovative in my role.

    (c) I have no opportunity to be innovative and do something creative.

15. (a) Others in the organization see my role as significant to their work.

    (b) I am a member of a task force or a committee.

    (c) I do not work on any committees.

16. (a) Hostility rather than co-operation is evident here.

    (b) I experience enough mutual help here.

    (c) People operate more in isolation here.

17. (a) I am able to contribute to the
company in my role.
  (b) I am able to serve society at large
in my role.
  (c) I wish I could do some useful
work in my role.

18. (a) I am able to influence relevant decisions.
  (b) I am sometimes consulted on
important matters.
  (c) I cannot make any independent
decisions.

19. (a) I learn a great deal in my role.
  b) I learn a few new things in my role.
  (c) I am involved in routine or unrelated
activities and have learned nothing.

20. (a) When people bring problems to
me, I tend to ask them to work
them out themselves.
  (b) I dislike being bothered with
interpersonal conflict.
  (c) I enjoy solving problems related
to my work.

(Source: R. Plant, *Managing Change and Making it Stick*, Fontana, 1987)

Appendix D   Challenge and Support

Challenge and support is one way of describing a culture. For this we have defined culture as *the way things are done around here*.

But Different People Like Different Things!

Challenge and support are experienced differently by different individuals. What I find challenging may be different for you. For instance, I may find that you questioning my opinion is quite challenging, but you disagreeing with it is even more so! But you may find questioning your views is rather supporting, it shows an interest in your view and you like the attention.

Security and the Need for Challenge or Support

People who are fairly secure will perform best. People very high or very low in security will not perform so well. If you are having a difficult time getting to grips with a new job, don't understand it well,

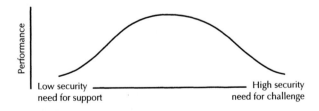

and wonder if you really did the right thing taking the job – then you are likely to feel less secure. On the other hand, if you've been in the job years, and can do everything before lunch, then you are likely to feel really secure. Neither of you will be performing to capacity.

So people very high or very low in security won't be performing as well as those in the middle.

If people at the high end are given **challenge**, and people at the low end are given **support**, they will move into the best performing zone.

Think of someone in your group or office who never seems pushed, always ready to pick up a task and work it. Think of another colleague who does the job and never volunteers for extra, and will never get any medals for industry. They seem impossible to motivate and quite content to work below par. What do these people need; challenge or support, to get them into the best place to perform well? It's people who feel both challenged and supported that perform well.

This model works for both organizations and individuals. If I'm feeling very stretched, my father is ill, many miles away, the washing machine has just bust, and I've been overlooked for promotion, I may need more support than challenge, to bring me to a good performance. Small 'hassles' seem to add together to give more strain than big, single life events.

High Performing Organizations

These often have a culture of high support and high challenge. They give both, and people in them seek both. However, no one can stay in the High Performance quadrant for ever, they will take rests or holidays, and move into one of the other quadrants, resting or accumulating energy, recharging their batteries for the next stage of High Performance.

In order to move into the High Performance quadrant it seems necessary to move through the high strain quadrant. I have not seen individuals or organizations make significant changes without some pain or strain. It seems a necessary part of change into High Performance.

See the diagram on the opposite page.

Challenge and Support

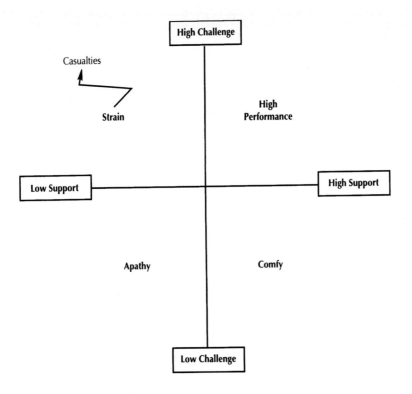

Index

self-assessment
    questionnaire 63–4,
    129–32
self-assessment tool,
    management 104–10
  checklist 122–3
  exercise 107–10;
    results 110–12
shock, stages of 70, 72–3
skills
  individuals: and change 31–3
  management arenas 112–14
  management skills
    checklist 111–12
  performance problems 15–17
soft systems methodology 52–8
  case study 53
strain 30, 74, 85, 134
strategic planning 42–3
stress 22, 25, 29–30, 45, 74,
  84–7
  literature on 30
  women managers 116
subordinates: management
  assessment 105–6
summative evaluation 51
support 82, 133–5
systemic approach: to
  performance problems 15–17

systems
  identifying 12–13
  nurses in 83–4
  readiness for change 14, 15,
    33–5, 82
  see also open systems

teams and teamwork 39–40, 44–5
  characteristics of
    functioning 44
  competition between 4–5
technical work 23, 42
territories, professional *see*
  boundaries
training needs:
  identifying 103–19
transactional leadership 37–8
transformational
  leadership 37–8, 40–1, 45
transition plans 20–1, 27–9, 33
  case study 100–1
  checklist 123, 124
transitions
  case studies 24, 25, 26, 28–9
  checklist 123
  letting go of old
    situation 22–4
  neutral zone 25–6
  new beginnings 26–9
  process of 21–2

uncertainty 25, 33, 44–5
unplanned change 77–9

vertical relationships 3–5
vision, future
  building 61–3
  shared 19

women
  in management 114–18; case
    study 117–18
  stress 86–7